LOVING FROM EMPTY

A Compassionate Guide for Exhausted Partners of Complex PTSD Survivors Facing the Stay-or-Leave Decision

Peggy Minnie Mayer

First Edition, 2026.

ISBN: 978-1-7645416-4-0

Table of Contents

Preface

Complex post-traumatic stress disorder occupies a particular place in the landscape of psychological research. Unlike single-incident PTSD, which arises from a discrete traumatic event, CPTSD develops in response to prolonged, repeated interpersonal trauma most often occurring in childhood, in captivity, or within relationships defined by coercive control. The diagnostic framework, formalized by Judith Herman in the early 1990s and subsequently codified as a distinct diagnosis in the World Health Organization's International Classification of Diseases, Eleventh Revision (ICD-11), recognizes that sustained exposure to interpersonal trauma produces a symptom profile that extends well beyond the re-experiencing, avoidance, and hyperarousal clusters of classical PTSD. CPTSD encompasses profound disturbances in affect regulation, self-concept, and relational functioning — disruptions that reach into every dimension of the survivor's intimate life and, by extension, into the lives of those closest to them.

The clinical and research literature on CPTSD has expanded significantly over the past three decades. Evidence-based treatments including Eye Movement Desensitization and Reprocessing (EMDR), Cognitive Processing Therapy (CPT), Internal Family Systems (IFS), somatic experiencing, and schema therapy have demonstrated measurable outcomes in reducing symptom severity and improving functional capacity for survivors. Neurobiological research has illuminated the mechanisms by which chronic trauma reshapes the stress response system, alters neural architecture, and produces the characteristic cycles of emotional dysregulation that define the condition. The field has made meaningful progress in understanding what CPTSD is, how it operates, and how survivors can be supported on the path toward recovery.

What the field has not adequately addressed is the experience of the intimate partner.

The literature on caregiver burden, secondary traumatic stress, and compassion fatigue has grown substantially within medical, military, and first-responder caregiving contexts. Research on the psychological toll of caring for individuals with chronic illness, cognitive decline, and combat-related PTSD has produced validated assessment instruments, evidence-based interventions, and a shared clinical vocabulary for the distress that caregivers experience. Yet the specific experience of the romantic partner navigating a CPTSD-affected relationship remains underrepresented in both the research literature and the consumer-facing resources available to the public.

This is a significant gap. The intimate partner of a CPTSD survivor occupies a role of extraordinary psychological complexity. They contend with the relational consequences of their partner's affect dysregulation the sudden withdrawals, the disproportionate emotional responses, the cycles of closeness and rupture that are characteristic of disrupted attachment systems. They learn to navigate trauma triggers that may be invisible, unpredictable, or rooted in experiences that predate the relationship entirely. They manage the practical and emotional labour of daily life while absorbing the secondary effects of a condition that, by its nature, distorts the very mechanisms of intimacy and trust upon which the relationship depends.

Over time, many partners experience a recognizable pattern of psychological consequences: identity erosion, chronic hypervigilance, emotional depletion, social isolation, the gradual abandonment of personal needs and aspirations, and a growing uncertainty about the boundary between compassion and self-sacrifice. These are not signs of weakness or codependency. They are the predictable psychological outcomes of sustained proximity to complex trauma within an intimate relational context, and they are documented in the emerging literature on partner-specific secondary traumatic stress.

This book was written to address the intersection that no existing resource adequately serves: the point at which a partner of a CPTSD survivor recognizes that the relationship, as it is currently functioning, may not be sustainable and must decide how to proceed.

The question of staying or leaving a trauma-affected relationship carries layers of complexity that standard relationship guidance is poorly equipped to address. It involves the neurobiological realities of trauma recovery and the timelines that govern meaningful change. It requires an accurate understanding of the distinction between trauma-driven behaviour and abusive dynamics — a distinction that is critical, nuanced, and frequently obscured in both clinical and popular literature. It demands reckoning with the weight of shared history, the particular guilt that accompanies the consideration of leaving someone whose suffering has identifiable origins, and the erosion of self-trust that makes confident decision-making feel impossible after years of prioritizing another person's needs.

The approach throughout this book is research-informed and clinically grounded. Each chapter draws on peer-reviewed literature in traumatic stress, attachment theory, relationship psychology, and neurobiological research, cited with accessible references. The reflection exercises are adapted from evidence-based therapeutic practices, including expressive writing protocols, values clarification methods, and structured self-assessment frameworks that have demonstrated efficacy in clinical settings. The case studies are composite illustrations drawn from common patterns documented in the clinical and therapeutic literature, designed to render abstract concepts tangible without representing any specific individual.

This book does not advocate for staying or for leaving. It advocates for clarity, self-knowledge, and informed decision-making. It proceeds from the position that a partner's wellbeing is not secondary to the wellbeing of the person with the diagnosis — that compassion and self-preservation are not mutually exclusive, and that a decision made from accurate information and self-awareness is qualitatively different from one made from exhaustion, guilt, or crisis.

The intended audience is any person in an intimate relationship with a CPTSD survivor who is questioning the sustainability of that relationship. It is also relevant for therapists, counsellors, and clinical practitioners who serve this population and seek a resource to recommend to the partners they encounter in their practice.

The goal of this work is to provide what partners have needed and not received: validation that their experience is real and that it matters, accurate information about the condition that shapes their daily lives, and a structured, evidence-informed framework for navigating one of the most difficult decisions a person in a loving relationship can face.

Peggy Minnie Mayer
Researcher and Author

Introduction

You may not have planned to buy this book.

Perhaps you reached a moment when the tension in your home felt heavier than usual. Perhaps you noticed how often you walk on eggshells, how carefully you measure your words, how quickly you silence your own feelings. Or perhaps nothing dramatic happened at all—just a quiet realization that something in you is tired.

You do not owe anyone an explanation for reading this book.

Loving someone who lives with Complex Post-Traumatic Stress Disorder (CPTSD) can be deeply meaningful. It can also be confusing, draining, and lonely. You may still see the person you fell in love with their kindness, their strength, their effort to survive what once hurt them. At the same time, you may be facing anger, withdrawal, unpredictability, or emotional distance that has slowly reshaped your days.

It is possible to care deeply and still feel worn down.
It is possible to stay and still question.
It is possible to think about leaving and still love them.

These truths can sit side by side.

This book is written for partners who find themselves standing in that in-between place. Not villains. Not saviors. Not martyrs. Just people trying to understand what is happening in their relationship and what it is costing them.

As you read, you will not be told what decision to make. You will not be judged for staying, and you will not be judged for considering leaving. Instead, you will be treated as someone whose experience matters.

Your needs matter.
Your exhaustion matters.
Your confusion matters.

And it is time they are taken seriously.

No Judgment Here

Reading a book with the words "stay or go" in its description takes courage. It means you've allowed yourself to consider a question that many partners of CPTSD survivors push away for months or even years. The fact that you're here says something about your willingness to face hard things honestly. That deserves acknowledgment, not shame.

Partners of people with CPTSD tend to share certain qualities. Research on caregiving partners in trauma affected relationships consistently identifies high empathy, strong loyalty, and deep emotional attunement as common traits (Dekel and Monson, 2010). These aren't weaknesses. They're the very qualities that made you a good partner in the first place. But they're also the qualities that make this particular situation so painful, because the same compassion that draws you toward your partner's suffering can slowly pull you away from your own needs.

If you've been the person who researches CPTSD symptoms at two in the morning, the one who explains your partner's behaviour to confused family members, the one who adjusts plans, absorbs mood shifts, and manages the emotional temperature of your household, then you already know what this costs. You know it in your body. You know it in the growing distance between who you used to be and who you are now.

And here's something that doesn't get said enough: the full range of what you feel is legitimate. Love and resentment can share the same breath. Hope and exhaustion can sit side by side without one cancelling the other. Devotion and depletion are not opposites. They can, and often do, show up together in relationships shaped by complex trauma.

Consider Elowen (name changed), who described her experience this way: "I love my husband. I also dread coming home most days. People act like those two things can't both be true. But they are. They're both completely true, and that's what makes this so hard." Elowen had spent six years supporting her partner through intensive trauma therapy. She celebrated every step forward. She also noticed that she had stopped seeing friends, stopped painting, and stopped sleeping through the night. The love was real. So was the cost.

You don't need to resolve that tension right now. You just need to know that this book will not ask you to pretend it doesn't show up.

A note on guilt: many partners feel deeply guilty for focusing on their own experience when their loved one is the one with the trauma history. Research on **secondary traumatic stress** (the stress that comes from close, sustained contact with someone who has experienced trauma) shows that partners are affected in measurable, documented ways (Figley, 2002). Your distress is not a competition with your partner's distress. It is its own real thing, and it deserves attention.

What This Book Offers

This book will not tell you what to do.

That might feel frustrating. If you're at a crisis point, you probably want someone to just give you the answer. Stay or go. Left or right. But anyone who claims to know the right answer for your specific relationship, your specific partner, and your specific life is offering you something they don't actually have.

What this book will do is give you a structure for thinking clearly about one of the hardest decisions a person can face. It provides information, not instructions. It offers perspective, not prescription.

Here's what this book is not:

It is not a case against your partner. Nothing in these pages positions people with CPTSD as villains, burdens, or lost causes. Complex PTSD is a serious condition that develops in response to prolonged, repeated trauma, most often in childhood (Herman, 1992). Your partner did not choose it. Their symptoms are not character flaws. And their capacity for healing is real, even when progress is painfully slow.

At the same time, this book does not romanticize trauma or treat it as something that automatically makes a person more interesting, more soulful, or more deserving of unconditional tolerance. Trauma explains behaviour. It does not excuse harm. That distinction will come up again and again throughout these chapters.

What this book is: a guide for helping you think clearly when everything feels foggy. A way to sort through what you're feeling, what's actually happening in your relationship, and what you need, so that whatever you decide comes from the most grounded, honest version of yourself.

And there's an important difference between making a decision and reaching a breaking point. A decision is something you arrive at with awareness. A breaking point is something that happens to you when you've run out of capacity. Dr. Judith Herman, whose work on complex trauma has shaped the field for over three decades, notes that recovery from trauma requires conditions of safety and choice (Herman, 1992). The same applies to you. Your choice about this relationship should come from a place of relative safety and clarity, not from the ragged edge of burnout.

Consider Bramwell (name changed), who left his partner of nine years during a particularly difficult week. "I didn't decide to leave," he said later. "I just couldn't take one more day. And then I was gone, and I didn't know if I'd actually wanted to go or if I'd just collapsed." Bramwell eventually returned to the relationship, but the unplanned departure created a new layer of rupture for both of them. His story is common. When partners leave from exhaustion rather than decision, neither person gets what they need from that ending.

This book aims to help you avoid that. Not by keeping you in the relationship or by pushing you out, but by helping you arrive at your own answer with your eyes open.

Choosing Versus Being Pushed

There is a version of "leaving" that isn't really a choice at all. It's what happens when a person stays past the point of capacity, gives until there is nothing left, and then exits not because they decided to, but because their body, their mind, or their spirit simply stopped cooperating.

This happens more often than people realize. Partners of CPTSD survivors frequently describe a slow erosion rather than a sudden crisis. The process has been compared to **compassion fatigue**, a term originally used to describe the cumulative emotional toll on healthcare workers and first responders who are repeatedly exposed to others' trauma (Figley, 2002). In intimate relationships, the same gradual wearing down occurs, but it happens in your home, in your bed, and with someone you love. That makes it harder to name and even harder to address.

Exhaustion has a way of mimicking clarity. When you're deeply depleted, the urge to leave can feel like a clear headed decision.

But genuine decision making requires a minimum level of cognitive and emotional resources. Research on decision making under stress shows that chronic stress impairs the prefrontal cortex functions responsible for weighing options, considering consequences, and thinking long term (Arnsten, 2009). In plain language: when you're running on empty, you're not in the best position to make life altering choices.

This doesn't mean the urge to leave is wrong. It might be exactly right. But it means the timing matters.

The goal is to make your decision (whatever it turns out to be) from the most resourced version of yourself. That might mean getting your own therapy before deciding. It might mean creating some temporary space. It might mean reading this book from start to finish and sitting with what comes up before taking action.

Making a conscious, informed choice is an act of respect toward yourself and toward your partner. If you stay, you want it to be because you've genuinely weighed the costs and possibilities, not because guilt held you in place. If you go, you want it to be because you've honestly assessed what's sustainable, not because you hit a wall at two in the morning.

Consider Aldwyn (name changed), who spent three months in individual therapy before making any decisions about his relationship. "My therapist told me something that changed how I thought about the whole thing," he said. "She told me that I didn't owe anyone a decision made from my worst moment. I could take time. I could think. And whatever I chose from that clearer place would be better for everyone, including my partner." Aldwyn eventually decided to stay in his relationship with significant structural changes. But the decision felt different because it was actually his, made from a grounded place rather than from crisis or guilt.

A note on timing: there is no perfect moment to make this kind of decision. If you wait for certainty, you'll wait forever. But there are better and worse conditions for clear thinking. You think more clearly when you've slept, when you have support, when you're not in the middle of an active conflict, and when you've had time to process your own emotions separately from your partner's. This book will help you create those conditions.

How to Read This Book

You can read this book from front to back. The chapters are designed to build on one another, moving from understanding what CPTSD is and how it affects relationships, through critical assessments of safety and realistic change, into the practical territory of what staying or leaving actually looks like.

But you can also go directly to whatever chapter feels most urgent. If you need to figure out whether what you're experiencing crosses a line into abuse, go to Chapter 3.0 now. If you need immediate support resources, turn to Chapter 9.0. There's no wrong way to move through this material, and the chapters include references to earlier and later sections so you can fill in context as you need it.

Throughout the book, you'll find reflection prompts and journaling questions woven into the text. These aren't busywork. Research on **expressive writing** shows that structured writing about emotionally difficult experiences can reduce psychological distress and improve clarity of thought (Pennebaker and Smyth, 2016). You don't have to complete every prompt. But if one catches your attention, give yourself permission to pause and sit with it. A notebook dedicated to this process can become one of the most useful tools you have.

One more thing, and it matters: if you are currently in danger (if your partner's behaviour includes physical violence, threats, or coercive control) please turn to Chapter 3.0 and the resources in

Chapter 9.0 before reading anything else. Your safety is the first priority, and the rest of this book will still be here when you're ready for it.

Before You Begin

This book holds space for two truths at once: your partner is struggling with something that was done to them, and you are struggling with the reality of what that means for your daily life. Neither truth cancels the other. Both deserve care.

Whatever you decide, this book asks only one thing of you: that you make room for your own experience. Not at your partner's expense. Not with cruelty or blame. But with the same compassion you've been extending to someone else, now turned, even briefly, toward yourself.

Chapter 1.At the Breaking Point

The breaking point rarely looks the way people imagine it. There's no dramatic scene, no single explosive argument, no moment where everything suddenly becomes clear. For most partners of people living with Complex Post Traumatic Stress Disorder, the breaking point is quieter than that. It's sitting in your car in the parking lot after work, not because you have anywhere to go, but because you need ten more minutes before walking through your own front door. It's realizing that you've been holding your breath since you heard the garage door open. It's the night you look at your partner across the dinner table and feel nothing at all, and that absence of feeling frightens you more than any argument ever did.

This chapter is about naming what that moment actually is. Not to dramatize it, not to push you toward any particular conclusion, but because naming something honestly is the first step toward doing anything about it.

The Moment Something Shifted

Most partners can identify a moment when the question first surfaced. Not necessarily the words "should I leave?" but something close. A feeling. A thought that showed up uninvited and wouldn't go away. For some, it arrives as a specific realization. For others, it's more like a slow dawning, the way you gradually notice that the temperature in a room has changed without being able to say exactly when.

What almost always follows that moment is guilt. Immediate, heavy guilt. Because the person you're questioning your future with is also the person you love, the person who has been through terrible things, the person whose trauma you understand on an intellectual level even when its daily effects leave you depleted.

This guilt is worth looking at, because it shapes everything that comes next. Research on guilt in caregiving relationships shows that guilt often functions as a self-silencing mechanism. Partners suppress their own needs and concerns because acknowledging them feels like a betrayal of the person they're caring for (Losada et al., 2010). The guilt doesn't mean your concerns are invalid. It means you care deeply, and caring deeply makes honest self-assessment feel dangerous.

So what do partners actually experience when they reach this point? Clinical literature and partner accounts consistently describe several common patterns.

Emotional numbness. Not depression exactly, but a protective flattening. You stop feeling the highs and the lows because feeling anything fully has become too costly. Numbness is your nervous system's way of saying: I can't process any more right now (Van der Kolk, 2014).

Chronic hypervigilance at home. You monitor your partner's mood the moment you hear their footsteps. You scan their face for signs of a bad day. You adjust your tone, your plans, your energy, all before a single word is spoken. This isn't anxiety in the clinical sense. It's an adaptive response to an unpredictable emotional environment, and it's exhausting.

Loss of identity. You used to have hobbies, opinions, friendships, a sense of who you were outside this relationship. Slowly, often without noticing, those things shrank. Your world got smaller. Your identity became "the partner who manages, supports, absorbs, and adapts."

Walking on eggshells as a way of life. Not occasionally. Not during bad weeks. Constantly. The feeling that any wrong word, wrong tone, or wrong topic could trigger a crisis has become the background noise of your daily life.

Consider Dunstan (name changed), who described reaching his breaking point after eight years with his partner. "There wasn't one big thing," he said. "It was more like I woke up one morning and realized I'd been anxious for so long that I'd forgotten what calm felt like. My doctor told me my blood pressure was dangerously high. I was forty-one. And something in my head just went: this is what it's doing to you. This is the price." Dunstan didn't leave that day. He didn't make any decisions for several months. But he stopped pretending everything was manageable.

One thing that deserves clear acknowledgment: saying "I can't do this anymore" is not the same as saying "I don't love them." Those two statements can be completely true at the same time. The capacity to endure something and the desire to be with someone operate on different tracks. Running out of endurance does not mean running out of love.

Reflection prompt: When did you first notice something had shifted for you? What did that moment feel like in your body, not just in your thoughts?

Small Ruptures That Add Up

Relationships affected by CPTSD dynamics rarely collapse all at once. They erode. The process is gradual enough that partners often struggle to explain what's wrong because there isn't one clear thing to point to. There are hundreds of small things, and each one felt survivable on its own.

The cancelled plans. The evening that was going well until a casual comment triggered a two-hour emotional spiral. The apology that came but somehow didn't land, because it was followed by an explanation of why the hurtful thing happened, which started to feel less like accountability and more like a redirect. The good week that ended without warning, leaving you confused about what went wrong and bracing for the next shift.

These are what relationship researchers call **micro-ruptures**: small breaks in connection that, individually, seem minor but cumulatively create significant damage to relationship trust and satisfaction (Gottman and Silver, 2015). In relationships where one partner has CPTSD, micro-ruptures often follow a particular pattern. The rupture occurs during a moment of emotional dysregulation. The partner with CPTSD may later feel deep shame about what happened, which can either lead to withdrawal or to a defensive posture that makes genuine repair difficult. The other partner absorbs the impact, forgives, adjusts, and moves on. Until the next time.

The accumulation of these small ruptures creates something that feels like erosion. The ground beneath the relationship gets thinner, and partners often don't realize how thin it's become until something relatively minor causes a disproportionate reaction, and they find themselves thinking: I can't do this one more time.

Consider Fenwick (name changed), who tracked what happened in his relationship over a single month. "I started writing things down because I felt like I was going crazy," he said. "In one month, we had eleven evenings where plans changed because of a mood shift. I cancelled on friends four times. I slept on the couch twice. We had two conversations that turned into arguments where I ended up apologizing even though I wasn't sure what I'd done wrong. And through all of that, there was no single event I could point to and say: that one. That's the problem. It was all of them together."

Partners often describe feeling that their pain isn't "valid enough" because they can't identify one clear incident. This is one of the most isolating aspects of being in a CPTSD-affected relationship. The damage is cumulative, but the world tends to understand suffering only when it comes with a clear cause. When you say "it's a thousand small things," people sometimes hear "it's not that bad."

It is that bad. Cumulative stress is well documented as a contributor to both psychological distress and physical health problems (Thoits, 2010). The absence of a single dramatic event does not reduce the impact. If anything, it makes the impact harder to process because there's no clear narrative to organize it around.

Reflection prompt: If you were to list the small ruptures from the past month, what would be on that list? Not the dramatic events, but the quiet accumulations?

What You're Actually Feeling

The emotional experience of reaching a breaking point in a CPTSD-affected relationship is layered and often contradictory. Three distinct but overlapping experiences deserve attention here, because they're frequently confused with each other.

Compassion fatigue is the gradual erosion of your ability to empathize. It doesn't mean you've become a cold person. It means your empathy reserves have been depleted by sustained, intense emotional demands. Figley (2002) described compassion fatigue as the "cost of caring" for those in close contact with traumatized individuals. In partner relationships, this often shows up as a startling moment when your partner is in distress and you feel... nothing. Or irritation. Or a thought you'd never say out loud: here we go again.

Burnout is broader. It's the exhaustion that comes from prolonged effort without adequate recovery. Burnout in caregiving relationships manifests as physical and emotional depletion, a growing sense of ineffectiveness ("nothing I do helps"), and detachment from the relationship itself (Maslach and Leiter, 2016).

Secondary traumatic stress goes further still. This is the development of trauma-like symptoms in someone who hasn't directly experienced trauma but has been closely and repeatedly exposed to someone else's traumatic material. Symptoms can include intrusive thoughts about your partner's trauma, hypervigilance, emotional numbing, and avoidance behaviours (Bride, 2007). If you've found yourself having nightmares about things that happened to your partner, or feeling triggered by situations that remind you of their trauma responses, this may be what you're experiencing.

These three experiences can overlap, and you may be dealing with more than one at the same time. Naming them matters because each one requires slightly different support, and because recognizing what's happening to you is itself a form of self-care.

Beyond these clinical patterns, partners at the breaking point often describe specific emotional cycles. The **guilt-resentment cycle** is among the most common: you feel resentment toward your partner, then immediate guilt for feeling resentful toward someone who is suffering, then you suppress the resentment, which builds until it surfaces again, bringing even more guilt. Round and round.

The **hope-crash cycle** is equally draining. A good period begins. Your partner is doing well. You start to relax, to hope, to believe things are changing. Then a regression hits, and the crash feels worse than if you'd never hoped at all. Over time, many partners stop allowing themselves to hope because the crash has become too painful.

And then there are the physical symptoms. Sleep disruption. Appetite changes. Chronic muscle tension, particularly in the jaw, shoulders, and back. Headaches. Stomach problems. Health issues that seem to appear from nowhere but are, in fact, your body's response to sustained stress. Research consistently links chronic interpersonal stress to measurable changes in immune function, cardiovascular health, and inflammatory markers (Kiecolt-Glaser et al., 2003).

Consider Godric (name changed), who went to his doctor about persistent chest tightness. "They ran every test. Heart was fine. Lungs were fine. My doctor finally asked me how things were at home, and I just started talking. I talked for twenty minutes. She listened and then said something I'll never forget: 'Your body is keeping score even if your mind is trying not to.' That was the first time anyone had connected what was happening in my relationship to what was happening in my body."

Reflection prompt: What is your body telling you right now? Where do you carry the stress of your relationship physically?

This Moment Is Information

Here is perhaps the most important reframing this chapter offers: your breaking point is not a failure. It is not evidence that you are selfish, weak, or incapable of love. It is information.

Your body and your mind are telling you something about what is and isn't sustainable. That information deserves to be heard, not argued with, not shamed away, and not dismissed because your partner's pain feels larger than yours.

Think of it this way: if a structural engineer found cracks in a building's foundation, nobody would call those cracks a moral failing. They would call them data. Important data that demands attention and a response. The cracks in your emotional foundation are the same kind of information. They tell you where the stress is concentrated. They tell you what needs to change, even if you don't yet know what that change looks like.

This doesn't mean you have to make a decision right now. It means you have to stop ignoring the data. The breaking point is an invitation, not a deadline. It's an invitation to stop operating on autopilot and to start paying attention to what you actually need.

The chapters ahead will help you do exactly that. Chapter 2.0 will give you a clear understanding of what CPTSD is and why it creates the patterns you've been living with. Chapter 3.0 will help you assess safety and distinguish between trauma-driven behaviour and abuse. And each chapter after that will move you closer to the clarity you need to make whatever decision is right for you.

But for now, just this: what you are feeling is real. What you are experiencing has a cost. And acknowledging that cost is not a betrayal of your partner. It is the beginning of telling yourself the truth.

The Honest Inventory

Before moving to the next chapter, take some time with this reflection exercise. Find a quiet moment, a notebook, and the willingness to be honest with yourself.

Answer these questions based on where you actually are right now, not where you wish you were or where you think you should be.

How would you describe your emotional state most days? Not on your best day and not on your worst. On an average Tuesday.

When was the last time you felt genuinely relaxed in your own home?

What parts of yourself have gotten smaller since this relationship began?

If a close friend described your daily experience back to you, what would you want to say to them?

What is your body telling you that you haven't been willing to hear?

There are no right answers. There is only honesty. And honesty, especially the kind that's been suppressed for a long time, is where everything begins.

Putting It Together

The breaking point is rarely one thing. It's the accumulation of small ruptures, the slow erosion of identity and energy, the physical toll of sustained emotional stress, and the growing gap between what you need and what your relationship can currently provide. Naming these experiences honestly is not an act of betrayal toward your partner. It is an act of respect toward yourself. Your distress has legitimate sources, measurable effects, and documented patterns. Whether you ultimately stay or go, acknowledging the reality of where you are right now is the necessary first step toward any kind of clarity. The chapters ahead will give you the information and structure to think through this decision carefully. But the foundation for all of it is the willingness to stop pretending that everything is fine when it isn't. You've already taken that step by reading this far.

Chapter 2 Understanding CPTSD

If you're living with a partner who has Complex Post Traumatic Stress Disorder, you've probably already done more research than most people ever will. You may know the terminology. You may understand, on a conceptual level, what happened to your partner and why they respond the way they do. But understanding something intellectually and living inside its daily effects are two entirely different experiences.

This chapter gives you a grounded, research-based picture of what CPTSD actually is, how it reshapes the brain and nervous system, and why it creates the specific relationship patterns you've been living with. This isn't about excusing your partner's behaviour. It's about making sense of patterns that otherwise feel personal, random, or deliberately hurtful. When you understand the mechanism, you stop spending your energy trying to decode individual incidents, and you start seeing the larger picture. That clarity matters, regardless of what you ultimately decide about your relationship.

What CPTSD Actually Is

Complex PTSD and standard PTSD share some features, but they are meaningfully different conditions with different origins, symptoms, and impacts on relationships. Standard PTSD typically develops after a single traumatic event or a discrete series of events: a car accident, a natural disaster, a combat experience. Complex PTSD develops in response to prolonged, repeated trauma, usually beginning in childhood, and usually occurring within relationships where the traumatized person could not escape (Herman, 1992).

That last part matters enormously for understanding your relationship. Your partner's trauma didn't come from an external event. It came from people. Often from the people who were supposed to protect and care for them. This means that the very thing your partner needs most (close, trusting human connection) is also the thing their nervous system has learned to treat as a source of danger.

The World Health Organization formally recognized CPTSD as a distinct diagnosis in the ICD-11, separating it from standard PTSD (World Health Organization, 2019). Beyond the core PTSD symptoms of re-experiencing, avoidance, and hyperarousal, CPTSD includes three additional clusters of symptoms that directly affect relationships.

Difficulties with emotional regulation. Your partner may experience intense emotional reactions that seem out of proportion to the situation, or they may shut down emotionally in ways that feel like withdrawal or punishment. Both responses reflect a nervous system that was shaped by environments where emotions were either dangerous or ignored.

Negative self-concept. People with CPTSD often carry deep, persistent beliefs that they are fundamentally flawed, unworthy of love, or permanently damaged. This isn't low self-esteem in the ordinary sense. It is a pervasive sense of shame that colours everything, including how they interpret your words, your silences, and your actions (Walker, 2013).

Disturbances in relationships. Difficulty trusting others, patterns of getting close then pulling away, trouble maintaining stable connections. These are not personality quirks. They are the predictable outcome of growing up in environments where closeness meant danger.

Reflection prompt: Which of these three additional symptom clusters do you recognize most clearly in your partner's daily behaviour? How does it show up in your interactions?

How Trauma Rewires Attachment

To understand why your relationship feels the way it does, you need to understand how trauma reshapes the attachment system. **Attachment theory**, developed by John Bowlby and later expanded by Mary Ainsworth, describes the way humans form emotional bonds with their primary caregivers in early childhood. These early patterns become templates for how we approach relationships throughout life (Bowlby, 1969).

When early caregiving is consistent, responsive, and safe, children develop what researchers call secure attachment. They learn that people can be relied upon, that their needs matter, and that closeness is generally safe. When early caregiving is frightening, neglectful, or chaotic, different attachment patterns form.

Many people with CPTSD develop what's known as **disorganized attachment** (sometimes called fearful-avoidant attachment). This is the attachment style most strongly linked to childhood trauma, and it creates a painful internal contradiction: the person simultaneously craves closeness and perceives closeness as threatening (Main and Hesse, 1990). The very person they want to turn to for comfort is also, in their internal wiring, a potential source of danger.

This is the push-pull dynamic that so many partners describe. Your partner reaches for you, then withdraws. They want intimacy but flinch when they get it. They test your loyalty in ways that feel exhausting or irrational. They may accuse you of not caring when you've been bending yourself in half to show that you do.

This isn't manipulation in the way most people understand it. It's a nervous system caught in an impossible bind. The part of your partner that wants love is constantly being overridden by the part that learned, through painful experience, that love is where the danger lives.

Consider Hadrian (name changed), whose partner would initiate closeness and then shut down within hours. "She'd ask me to hold her, and I'd feel so relieved because it meant she was letting me in. Then an hour later, she'd be cold and distant, and if I asked what happened, she'd say she needed space. I used to take it personally every single time. Once I understood the disorganized attachment piece, I stopped blaming myself. But I'll be honest: understanding it didn't make it hurt less."

Hadrian's experience captures something important. Understanding the attachment dynamics at play gives you a frame for what's happening. It removes the confusion of "what did I do wrong?" But it does not remove the emotional impact of living inside that pattern day after day.

Reflection prompt: When you think about the push-pull pattern in your relationship, what does the "push" look like and what does the "pull" look like? How do you typically respond to each?

The Nervous System in the Room

Every interaction you have with your partner involves two nervous systems, not just two people. And when one of those nervous systems has been shaped by complex trauma, the dynamics shift in ways that affect everything.

Polyvagal theory, developed by Dr. Stephen Porges, offers a useful way to understand this (Porges, 2011). In simple terms, your nervous system operates in different states depending on how safe or threatened it feels. When you feel safe, you're in a ventral vagal state: calm, connected, able to engage. When you detect a threat, your system shifts into sympathetic activation: fight (anger, aggression) or flight (anxiety, escape). If the threat feels overwhelming or inescapable, you drop into a dorsal vagal state: freeze (shutdown, numbness, dissociation) or fawn (people-pleasing, submitting to avoid conflict).

People with CPTSD have nervous systems with a much lower threshold for perceiving threat. Something that registers as mildly annoying to you (a changed plan, a slightly frustrated tone of voice, a moment of distraction during conversation) can register as a survival-level threat to your partner's nervous system. This isn't choice. It isn't drama. It's neurobiology. Their threat detection system was calibrated in an environment where small cues really did signal danger, and that calibration doesn't automatically reset just because the environment has changed (Van der Kolk, 2014).

This is why your partner's reactions can seem wildly out of proportion to the trigger. When they respond with rage to a comment about dishes, or shut down completely because you forgot to text back within an hour, they are not (in most cases) responding to the dishes or the text. They are responding to what those things mean in the internal world shaped by their trauma: you don't care, I'm not important, this person will leave me too.

Emotional flashbacks are a central feature of CPTSD and one of the hardest for partners to recognize. Unlike the flashbacks associated with standard PTSD (which typically involve visual memories or sensory re-experiencing), emotional flashbacks are a sudden regression to the emotional state of the traumatized child. There may be no visual memory at all. Your partner simply feels, with full intensity, the terror, helplessness, or abandonment they experienced in childhood (Walker, 2013). They may not even know a flashback is happening. They just know they suddenly feel terrible, and you're the person standing in front of them.

The **window of tolerance** is a concept developed by Dr. Dan Siegel that describes the zone within which a person can experience emotions without becoming overwhelmed or shutting down (Siegel, 2012). People with CPTSD typically have a much narrower window of tolerance than those without trauma histories. This means they're pushed outside their capacity to cope by stressors that wouldn't faze someone with a wider window. When your partner is outside their window of tolerance, their capacity for rational conversation, empathy, and perspective-taking drops dramatically.

And here's something that rarely gets talked about: your nervous system has been adapting to theirs. If you've been living with a partner whose nervous system is frequently dysregulated, your own system has almost certainly shifted. You may have become hypervigilant (constantly scanning for signs of their mood changes). You may have developed your own fawn response (automatically adjusting yourself to prevent their distress). Your window of tolerance may have narrowed too. This is called **co-dysregulation**, and it's a normal neurobiological response to sustained proximity to someone in chronic distress (Porges, 2011).

Consider Ivor (name changed), who realized his own nervous system had changed after his partner began CPTSD treatment. "Once she started getting more stable, I expected to feel relief. Instead, I felt more anxious. My therapist explained that my system had gotten used to being on high alert, and now that the threat level was dropping, my body didn't know what to do with the quiet. I'd spent so many years scanning for danger signals that I didn't know how to just be in a room without monitoring everything."

Reflection prompt: How has your own nervous system changed since being in this relationship? Do you notice hypervigilance, people-pleasing, or shutting down in situations that wouldn't have affected you before?

Beneath the Behaviour

One of the hardest parts of loving someone with CPTSD is that
what you see on the surface rarely reflects what's happening
underneath. The iceberg metaphor is useful here: the behaviour
you witness (the anger, the withdrawal, the accusations, the self-
sabotage) is only the visible portion. Beneath the waterline is a
massive structure of shame, fear, grief, and self-loathing that
drives everything above it.

Shame storms are a particularly disorienting experience for
partners. A shame storm is an intense, overwhelming flood of
shame that can be triggered by surprisingly minor events: a
perceived criticism, a moment of vulnerability, a mistake.
During a shame storm, your partner's internal experience is
consumed by the conviction that they are fundamentally bad,
unlovable, or worthless. The behaviours this drives can vary
widely. Some people lash out (rage as a defence against shame).
Some withdraw completely (hiding from the source of shame).
Some blame-shift (redirecting the shame onto you). Some self-
sabotage (confirming the belief that they don't deserve good
things).

Pete Walker, whose clinical work on CPTSD has been
influential in the field, describes the **inner critic** as one of the
core features of complex trauma. The inner critic is an
internalized voice of the abusive or neglectful caregiver, now
operating inside your partner's mind as a relentless source of
self-attack (Walker, 2013). When the inner critic is active, your
partner may hear everything you say through a filter of assumed
criticism. A neutral statement ("I'm tired") becomes an
accusation ("you exhaust me"). A request for space becomes
abandonment. An honest conversation about the relationship
becomes confirmation that they're unlovable.

This distortion is not intentional. Your partner is not choosing to
misinterpret you. They are processing your words through a

system that was trained, through years of painful experience, to expect rejection and harm from the people closest to them.

And healing from all of this is not linear. Your partner may have months of genuine progress followed by what feels like a sudden regression. This pattern of improvement and setback is well documented in trauma recovery literature and is considered normal, not a sign of failure (Herman, 1992). But for partners, the regressions can feel devastating. You invest in the progress, you allow yourself to hope, and then the old patterns resurface and it feels like starting over.

Consider Jory (name changed), whose partner had been in weekly trauma therapy for two years. "Year one was rough but we could see the progress. She was calmer, more communicative, more present. Year two started great and then she hit some material in therapy that sent her spiraling. For about three months, it felt like we were back at square one. I had to learn that the spiral didn't erase the progress. But living through it, in the moment? That distinction was hard to hold onto."

Reflection prompt: Can you think of a recent situation where your partner's visible behaviour probably didn't match what was happening inside them? What might have been beneath the surface?

Why Understanding Isn't Enough

Everything in this chapter so far has been about giving you information. And that information is genuinely useful. When you understand what CPTSD does to a person's attachment system, nervous system, and internal world, you stop personalizing things that were never really about you. You gain a vocabulary for what's happening. You see patterns instead of random cruelty.

But here's the part that needs to be said clearly: understanding why your partner does what they do does not undo the impact of what they do.

Empathy is a beautiful human quality. It is also not a relationship strategy. You can understand, on a deep level, that your partner's rage comes from a place of terrified shame, and you can still be damaged by that rage. You can know that their withdrawal is a trauma response, not a punishment, and still feel the loneliness of a partner who disappears for days at a time. Knowledge explains. It does not heal the wound in you.

One of the most common traps partners fall into is becoming the unlicensed therapist. You read the books. You learn the language. You start managing your partner's triggers, interpreting their behaviour for friends and family, and coaching them through emotional crises. You become so skilled at understanding their inner world that you lose contact with your own. Research on role confusion in caregiving relationships suggests that when partners take on therapeutic functions, relationship satisfaction declines for both people (Benazon and Coyne, 2000).

Your partner needs a therapist. That therapist is not you. Your role in this relationship is partner, not clinician. And maintaining that boundary is not cold or uncaring. It is one of the most important things you can do for both of you.

Compassion and boundaries are not opposites. You can hold deep compassion for what your partner has endured and still say: this is what I need, this is what I can tolerate, and this is where my limit falls. In fact, the research on boundaries in trauma-affected relationships consistently shows that clear, consistent boundaries improve outcomes for both partners (Johnson, 2019). Boundaries don't damage the relationship. The absence of boundaries does.

Reflection prompt: In what ways have you taken on the role of therapist, interpreter, or emotional manager for your partner? What would it look like to step back from that role?

Mapping the Pattern

Before moving to the next chapter, spend some time with this reflection exercise. The goal is to identify the recurring cycles in your relationship and to see where CPTSD dynamics may be driving them.

Think of a recent conflict or difficult period. Write down what happened, step by step, from trigger to resolution (or non-resolution).

Now look at the sequence. Where did the CPTSD dynamics you've learned about in this chapter appear? Was there a moment of emotional flashback? A shame storm? A push-pull cycle? A shift outside the window of tolerance?

How did you respond at each stage? Did you accommodate, withdraw, escalate, or freeze?

What was the outcome? Did genuine repair happen, or did the incident get absorbed without resolution?

How many times has a similar cycle played out in the past six months?

This exercise isn't about assigning blame. It's about seeing the pattern from enough distance to recognize it as a pattern, not as a series of isolated incidents. The patterns are the information. And once you can see them clearly, you're in a much better position to decide what, if anything, you want to do about them.

As we move into Chapter 3.0, we'll address one of the most difficult and necessary questions in this entire book: how to tell the difference between behaviour that is driven by trauma and behaviour that crosses the line into abuse. That chapter requires the foundation you've built here, so carry what you've learned forward. It will matter.

Essential Points to Remember

CPTSD is not the same as standard PTSD. It develops from prolonged, repeated trauma, usually in childhood, and it specifically affects emotional regulation, self-concept, and the ability to maintain close relationships. Your partner's nervous system was calibrated in a dangerous environment, and that calibration shapes how they perceive and respond to you, often triggering survival responses in situations that feel safe to you. Disorganized attachment, emotional flashbacks, shame storms, and the inner critic are all features of CPTSD that directly affect relationship dynamics. Your own nervous system has likely adapted in response to your partner's, and those changes in you also deserve attention. Understanding CPTSD gives you a clearer picture of what's happening, but understanding alone does not repair the impact on you. Compassion and boundaries are both necessary, and your role is partner, not therapist. The patterns you've identified in this chapter will form the basis for the harder assessments ahead.

Chapter 3 Trauma or Abuse

This may be the hardest chapter in this book to read. It may also be the most necessary.

If you've spent time in CPTSD communities, online forums, or therapy waiting rooms, you've likely absorbed a particular message: your partner's behaviour is a symptom of their trauma, and with enough understanding, patience, and the right treatment, things will get better. That message is often true. But it is not always true. And the difference matters more than almost anything else in this book.

There is a line between a partner who is struggling with the effects of complex trauma and a partner whose behaviour has crossed into abuse. That line can be blurry. It can shift. It can be hard to see when you're standing inside the relationship rather than looking at it from a safe distance. But it is there, and you deserve to know where it falls in your situation.

This chapter will help you make that assessment. Not by diagnosing your partner, not by labelling your relationship, but by giving you a clear, research-informed set of distinctions that allow you to see what's actually happening. Trauma explains behaviour. It does not excuse harm. Both of those things are true, and holding them together is what this chapter asks you to do.

Why This Chapter Is Here

The discomfort you may feel right now, even reading these words, is telling. Many partners of CPTSD survivors resist the idea that their relationship could involve abuse. The resistance comes from multiple directions.

From inside: you love this person. You've seen their pain. You know what was done to them. Calling their behaviour "abusive" feels like adding another wound to someone who's already been wounded enough.

From the CPTSD community: well-meaning support spaces sometimes create an unintentional dynamic where the person with the trauma diagnosis receives all the compassion, and the partner's experience is treated as secondary. Partners who raise concerns about harmful behaviour can be told they're being unsupportive, that they need to "educate themselves more," or that they're retraumatizing their partner by having needs. Research on online mental health communities confirms that these spaces can inadvertently discourage critical assessment of relationship dynamics by framing all behaviour through the lens of the diagnosis (Prescott and Mackie, 2017).

From culture: there's a broader narrative that says if someone has a mental health condition, holding them accountable is unkind. This narrative confuses accountability with punishment. They are not the same thing.

Here is something that needs to be said plainly: CPTSD and abusive behaviour can coexist in the same person. Having a trauma history does not make someone incapable of being harmful. Some people who were abused go on to treat others with extraordinary gentleness. Some go on to replicate patterns of harm. Most fall somewhere in between. The diagnosis tells you what shaped your partner. It does not automatically tell you if your partner is safe to be with.

The question "is this trauma or abuse?" is not a betrayal. It is a form of due diligence. And your willingness to ask it honestly is an act of care toward yourself that you have every right to perform.

Telling the Difference

The distinction between trauma-driven behaviour and abusive behaviour is not always obvious, but it is real. Researchers and clinicians who work at the intersection of trauma and intimate partner violence have identified several key markers that help differentiate the two (Dutton, 2007; Johnson, 2008).

Here are the questions that matter most.

What happens after the harmful behaviour? When your partner says or does something hurtful, what follows? A person whose behaviour is driven by trauma dysregulation will typically show genuine remorse once they've returned to a regulated state. They may feel deep shame (which can itself be destabilizing). They will generally acknowledge that what happened was not okay. A person whose behaviour is abusive will more often justify, minimize, or blame you for provoking them. The distinction is not perfect (some abusive individuals show performative remorse), but the pattern over time is telling.

Is there willingness to get help? A trauma-driven partner who is causing harm will, when confronted honestly, generally show some willingness to seek professional support. They may be afraid of therapy. They may resist initially. But the trajectory, over time, is toward engagement with treatment. An abusive partner will more often refuse to acknowledge a problem, attend one or two sessions and then stop, or use the language of therapy to further control the relationship ("my therapist said you're the one with the problem").

When does the behaviour occur? This is one of the most important distinctions. Trauma-driven behaviour tends to occur during states of dysregulation: emotional flashbacks, shame storms, moments when the nervous system is activated beyond the window of tolerance. The person may appear confused, overwhelmed, or frightened during and after. Abusive behaviour, by contrast, often occurs during calm, controlled moments. If your partner can modulate their behaviour depending on who is watching (gentle with others, harmful with you), that is significant information (Bancroft, 2002).

Is your world getting smaller? Over time, does the relationship give you more room to be yourself, or less? Do you see friends less often? Have you stopped doing things you used to enjoy? Do you monitor your words, your tone, your appearance, your schedule to avoid conflict? Research on coercive control identifies the progressive restriction of a partner's autonomy as one of the most reliable indicators of abuse, even in the absence of physical violence (Stark, 2007).

Can your partner take accountability for impact? There is a difference between intent and impact. Your partner may not have intended to hurt you. But if they cannot acknowledge that they did hurt you, regardless of their intent, that is a significant relational failure. Trauma-driven partners can, with support, learn to separate their intent from their impact and take responsibility for both. Partners engaging in abusive dynamics will more often insist that their intent is the only thing that matters, or will turn the conversation back to their own pain in ways that erase yours.

Consider Kenrick (name changed), who spent years distinguishing between his partner's trauma responses and a growing pattern of control. "For a long time, I could tell the difference. When she was triggered, it looked different. She'd get this look in her eyes, like she wasn't really seeing me. Those moments were hard, but I could understand them. What started worrying me was the other stuff. The calm conversations where she'd tell me which friends I shouldn't see. The way she'd go through my phone and frame it as needing reassurance. The fact that she could hold it together perfectly at work and with friends but would come home and tear me apart. That pattern is what finally made me see it wasn't all trauma."

It's worth noting that trauma responses and abusive dynamics can alternate in the same relationship, even in the same week. You don't need to categorize every single interaction. What matters is the overall pattern and whether, on balance, your partner's behaviour is something they're working to change or something they're using their diagnosis to justify.

Patterns that suggest trauma responses: emotional flooding during conflict, shutting down or withdrawing when overwhelmed, difficulty staying present during hard conversations, people-pleasing followed by resentment, disproportionate reactions to perceived rejection or abandonment, genuine distress about their own behaviour after the fact.

Patterns that suggest abuse: controlling who you see and when, monitoring your communications, using financial resources as leverage, intimidation (even without physical contact), threats to harm themselves if you set boundaries or leave, weaponizing information you shared in vulnerability, gaslighting (systematically making you doubt your own perceptions), and any form of physical violence.

Reflection prompt: Looking at the distinctions above, where do your partner's most concerning behaviours fall? Do you see a consistent pattern, or does it shift?

When Explaining Becomes Excusing

One of the most common traps in CPTSD relationships is the gradual slide from compassionate understanding to enabling. You understand why your partner behaves the way they do. You can trace the behaviour back to the trauma. And that understanding, which began as an act of empathy, slowly becomes a reason to tolerate things that are not tolerable.

The phrase "they can't help it" deserves careful examination. In the acute moment of a trauma flashback or a severe shame spiral, your partner genuinely may not have full control over their nervous system response. That is real. But "can't help it in this moment" is very different from "can't help it ever" or "won't get help for it."

Your partner's capacity for regulation can improve with appropriate treatment. If they are in consistent therapy, actively working on their responses, and showing progress over time (even with setbacks), then the "can't help it" framing carries weight. If they are not in treatment, refuse to engage with treatment, or use their diagnosis as a blanket explanation for ongoing harm without making any effort to change, then "can't help it" has become "won't address it." And that distinction changes the equation.

The CPTSD diagnosis itself can sometimes be co-opted in ways that silence legitimate concerns. Dr. Lundy Bancroft, whose work on abusive relationship dynamics has been widely influential, notes that some individuals use therapeutic language and diagnostic labels to avoid accountability (Bancroft, 2002). If your partner responds to your concerns by saying "you're triggering me," "you need to learn about trauma," or "my therapist says you should be more supportive," pay attention to whether these statements are genuine expressions of need or tools for shutting down conversations that hold them accountable.

Here's a question that can cut through a lot of confusion: if a close friend described your exact situation to you, word for word, what would you tell them?

Most partners, when they honestly consider this question, discover that their advice to a friend would be quite different from the narrative they've constructed for themselves. That gap between what you'd tell someone you love and what you're willing to accept for yourself is worth noticing.

Consider Larkin (name changed), who had this experience in a support group. "Someone else in the group described almost exactly what I was going through. And I was horrified for her. I wanted to shake her and say, 'You deserve better than this.' Then I realized I was living the same situation and making every excuse in the book for it. The same behaviour that outraged me in someone else's story was somehow acceptable in mine because I understood the reasons behind it."

Reflection prompt: What are you currently explaining away that, if a friend described it to you, would concern you?

Red Lines and Safety

Some things are not negotiable, regardless of the explanation behind them. This section addresses the boundaries that should never be crossed, even in the context of complex trauma.

Physical violence of any kind. Hitting, shoving, grabbing, throwing objects at you, blocking your exit from a room. Trauma may explain why someone becomes physically aggressive. It does not make physical violence acceptable, and it does not make you obligated to remain in its path. Research is unequivocal: physical violence in intimate relationships tends to escalate over time, not decrease (Walker, 2009).

Threats. Threats to harm you, to harm themselves if you leave, to take your children, to destroy your reputation. Threats are a form of coercive control, and their purpose is to restrict your freedom of action. If your partner threatens self-harm when you try to set boundaries or discuss leaving, this is a crisis that requires professional intervention, not a reason for you to abandon your own needs.

Coercive control. This is a pattern of behaviour that systematically strips away your autonomy, dignity, and independence. It can include monitoring your movements, controlling finances, isolating you from support networks, dictating your appearance, and creating an environment of fear and dependency. Coercive control is recognized as a form of domestic abuse in multiple legal jurisdictions and is associated with serious harm to victims (Stark, 2007).

Harm to children. If there are children in your household and they are being harmed, frightened, or exposed to ongoing abuse or severe dysregulation, their safety takes precedence. Children absorb relational dynamics even when they are not the direct target, and chronic exposure to an unstable or frightening home environment has well-documented effects on child development (Lieberman and Van Horn, 2008).

If any of the above are present in your relationship, please turn to Chapter 9.0 for immediate support resources. You do not need to figure this out on your own, and you do not need to read the rest of this book before taking action.

For those whose situations fall on a spectrum rather than at an extreme, a structured safety assessment can help clarify where you stand. Ask yourself:

Do you feel physically safe in your home most of the time?

Can you express disagreement without fear of retaliation?

Do you have access to your own finances?

Are you free to see friends and family without needing permission or facing consequences?

Can you make decisions about your own body, health, and schedule?

If you answered no to any of these, your situation may involve dynamics that go beyond trauma-driven difficulty and into territory that requires professional safety planning.

Why leaving an abusive relationship with a traumatized partner requires specific care: your partner's trauma history adds layers of complexity to the leaving process. They may escalate when they sense abandonment. They may genuinely be at risk of self-harm. They may use their vulnerability to pull you back. None of this means you should stay. But it does mean that if you decide to leave, doing so with professional support (a therapist, a domestic violence advocate, a safety plan) is not optional. It is essential. More on this in Chapter 8.0.

The Grey Zone

Many partners reading this chapter will not find themselves at either end of the spectrum. Their relationship doesn't involve clear-cut abuse. But it also isn't okay. They live in the grey zone: a space where ongoing dynamics cause real, cumulative harm without any single behaviour that clearly crosses a line.

The concept of **relational harm** is useful here. Relational harm refers to the damage done by sustained patterns of interaction that erode wellbeing, even when no individual incident constitutes abuse (Brassard et al., 2015). This can include chronic emotional unavailability, repeated ruptures without repair, ongoing invalidation of your experience, or a relational dynamic where your needs are consistently treated as secondary.

Living in the grey zone is, in some ways, harder than living with clear abuse. When the situation is clearly dangerous, the path forward (however difficult) is also clear: get to safety. When the situation is ambiguous, you're left making judgment calls with incomplete information, and the doubt can be paralyzing.

Here's what the grey zone requires: trusting your own experience. Not your analysis. Not your understanding of their diagnosis. Not the opinions of friends or online communities. Your experience. If your daily life in this relationship is causing you measurable harm (physical symptoms, mental health decline, loss of identity, chronic distress), then the harm is real regardless of whether it fits a particular category.

As we discussed in Chapter 1.0, your breaking point is information. The grey zone doesn't need a label to deserve your attention. It just needs honesty.

Consider Merrick (name changed), who spent over a year trying to figure out whether his partner's behaviour qualified as abuse. "I read every article, every checklist, every forum post. Some days I'd convince myself it was abuse, and other days I'd talk myself out of it. My therapist finally said something that changed my thinking. She said, 'You don't need a label to justify taking care of yourself. The question isn't whether this meets the definition of abuse. The question is whether this is the life you want to be living.'"

Reflection prompt: If you set aside the question of labels entirely, how would you describe the quality of your daily life in this relationship?

The Behaviour Audit

This reflection exercise asks you to look at specific behaviours with honesty and structure. It is not designed to produce a verdict. It is designed to produce clarity.

Choose three to five specific behaviours from your partner that concern you most. For each one, write down the following:

What is the behaviour? Describe it specifically, not in general terms. Not "they get angry" but "when I bring up something that bothers me, they raise their voice, tell me I'm too sensitive, and leave the room."

How often does it happen? Once a month? Weekly? Daily?

What is the context? Does it occur during moments of clear dysregulation (flashback, panic, shame spiral) or during calm interactions?

What happens afterward? Is there genuine remorse, or justification? Does repair happen?

What is the impact on you? On any children in the household?

Has this behaviour changed over time? Getting better, staying the same, or getting worse?

Look at what you've written. You don't need to draw a conclusion today. But the information is now outside of your head and on paper, where it's harder to minimize or reframe. Let it sit. Let it speak for itself. And carry what it tells you into the chapters ahead.

What This Means

The line between trauma-driven behaviour and abuse is not always sharp, but it is always worth looking for. Your partner's trauma history is real, and it shapes their behaviour in ways that deserve compassion. At the same time, compassion does not require you to tolerate harm. The key distinctions (remorse versus justification, willingness to seek help, context of the behaviour, impact on your autonomy, and capacity for accountability) give you a way to assess what you're actually living with. If your situation involves clear red lines, your safety is the priority and professional support is essential. If you're in the grey zone, trust your own experience and take seriously the cumulative harm that ongoing patterns can cause. Whatever the answer, asking the question honestly is not a betrayal. It is one of the most courageous things a partner can do.

Chapter 4 What Can Actually Change

Hope is a complicated thing in CPTSD relationships. Too much of it keeps you waiting for a version of your partner that may never arrive. Too little of it closes doors that might still be worth opening. What you need is not more hope or less hope. What you need is accurate hope: a clear, evidence-based picture of what CPTSD recovery actually looks like, what it requires, and what it can and cannot change about your relationship.

This chapter gives you that picture. It won't promise miracles, and it won't tell you that change is impossible. It will tell you what the research says about recovery, what the difference is between willingness and capacity, and how to assess whether the changes you're waiting for are realistic or not. Whatever you decide about your relationship, you deserve to make that decision based on what's actually true rather than on wishful thinking or despair.

The Recovery Landscape

CPTSD recovery is real. It happens. People with complex trauma histories do heal, build stable relationships, and develop the capacity for emotional regulation that their early environments denied them. But recovery from CPTSD is not what many people imagine it to be.

It is not a cure. There is no point at which your partner's trauma history disappears or stops influencing them entirely. Recovery is better understood as a fundamental rewiring of the nervous system, the attachment system, and the internal belief structures that trauma created. That rewiring is possible, but it takes time, consistent effort, and professional support (Cloitre et al., 2011).

Several evidence-based treatments have shown measurable results for CPTSD.

Eye Movement Desensitization and Reprocessing (EMDR) helps the brain reprocess traumatic memories so they no longer trigger the same intensity of emotional response. Research supports its effectiveness for complex trauma, though treatment typically requires more sessions than for single-incident PTSD (Shapiro, 2018).

Cognitive Processing Therapy (CPT) works directly on the distorted beliefs that trauma creates ("I'm worthless," "no one can be trusted," "the world is dangerous"). CPT helps people identify and challenge these beliefs systematically (Resick et al., 2017).

Internal Family Systems (IFS) treats the mind as composed of different "parts," each carrying different roles and burdens. For CPTSD survivors, IFS can help access and heal the wounded parts without overwhelming the system as a whole (Schwartz, 2021).

Somatic Experiencing addresses trauma stored in the body, working with physical sensations and nervous system responses rather than focusing exclusively on cognitive processing. This approach can be particularly useful for survivors whose trauma is pre-verbal or deeply body-based (Levine, 2010).

Schema Therapy identifies and works with deeply held patterns (called schemas) that formed in response to unmet childhood needs. For CPTSD, this approach addresses the core belief systems that drive relational difficulties (Young et al., 2003).

The realistic timeline for meaningful change is months to years, not weeks. A phased approach to trauma treatment is generally recommended: first stabilization (learning to regulate emotions and establish safety), then processing (working through the

traumatic material), then integration (rebuilding life patterns).
Dr. Judith Herman's three-stage model remains foundational in
the field and emphasizes that skipping the stabilization phase
often leads to retraumatization rather than recovery (Herman,
1992).

And here's something that partners need to hear: "better" may
not look the way you've been imagining. Recovery doesn't mean
your partner becomes someone who never gets triggered, never
has a bad day, and never struggles with the effects of their
history. It means they develop more capacity to manage their
responses, more ability to repair after ruptures, and more
awareness of how their behaviour affects you. That's real,
meaningful change. But it's different from the fantasy of a
partner whose trauma simply vanishes.

*Reflection prompt: When you imagine your partner "getting
better," what does that picture look like? How much of that
picture is realistic based on what you've just read?*

The Weight of Willingness

Of all the factors that predict whether a person with CPTSD will
make meaningful progress in recovery, willingness is the most
important. Not intelligence, not severity of symptoms, not the
quality of the therapist (though that matters too). Willingness.
The consistent, sustained commitment to doing the difficult
work of healing.

What willingness looks like in practice:

Consistent therapy attendance. Not starting and stopping. Not
going for a few weeks after a crisis and then drifting away.
Regular, ongoing engagement with a qualified trauma therapist.

Medication compliance, if medication has been prescribed.
Some people with CPTSD benefit from medication to manage

symptoms like severe anxiety, depression, or sleep disruption. Willingness includes taking prescribed medication as directed and communicating honestly with prescribers about its effects.

Accountability. This means being able to say, after a difficult incident, "I know my behaviour hurt you, and that's on me to work on," without immediately redirecting to their own pain. Accountability doesn't require perfection. It requires the consistent effort to own impact separately from intent.

Effort between sessions. Therapy is one hour a week (or less). What happens in the other 167 hours matters more. Willingness shows up in the daily work: using coping strategies, practicing the skills learned in therapy, reading relevant materials, and making conscious choices to respond differently even when it's hard.

What unwillingness looks like is equally important to recognize:

Lip service without follow-through. Agreeing to get help but never making the appointment. Starting therapy and quitting after a few sessions. Saying "I know I need to work on this" repeatedly without any visible change in behaviour.

Blaming you for their symptoms. "I wouldn't get triggered if you didn't..." is not accountability. It is a redirect that places the burden of their regulation on you.

Using the diagnosis as a shield. "I have CPTSD, so you can't expect me to..." may be legitimate in specific, acute moments. When it becomes a blanket justification for ongoing harm, it has shifted from explanation to excuse. As we covered in Chapter 3.0, that distinction matters.

The difference between "not ready yet" and "never going to be ready" is genuinely difficult to assess. Some people need time to build the courage and trust necessary to engage with trauma treatment. That's understandable. But "not ready" has a shelf life. If your partner has been "not ready" for years, with no movement toward readiness, the distinction between "not yet" and "not ever" becomes academic. Research on readiness for change suggests that external pressure (such as a partner reaching a breaking point) can sometimes catalyze movement, but only if the internal motivation is already present at some level (Prochaska and DiClemente, 1983).

Consider Oswin (name changed), who waited four years for his partner to engage with therapy. "She'd say she was going to find a therapist, and I'd feel this rush of relief. Then nothing would happen. After a crisis, she'd go for three or four sessions, start feeling a bit better, and stop. It took me a long time to see the pattern for what it was. She wasn't building toward something. She was managing crises just enough to stay in the same place."

Reflection prompt: When you look at your partner's behaviour over the past year, do you see evidence of genuine willingness to change, or a pattern of partial engagement followed by retreat?

Willingness Versus Capacity

Here is one of the most painful realities in CPTSD relationships: some people are genuinely willing but not yet capable. They want to change. They mean it when they say they're sorry. They go to therapy. They try. And they still repeat the same patterns, because the neurobiological effects of complex trauma don't yield to good intentions alone.

Early in recovery, the brain is still operating with a hijacked threat detection system, a narrow window of tolerance, and deeply grooved neural pathways that default to old survival responses under stress. Research on neuroplasticity confirms that these pathways can change, but the process is gradual and requires sustained, consistent effort over time (Davidson and McEwen, 2012). Your partner may genuinely want to respond differently to you in a moment of conflict and find that their body and brain override that intention before they're even aware of what's happening.

This is not an excuse. It is a description of what the brain does in early and mid-recovery. And it creates an agonizing dilemma for partners: how long do you wait for capacity to catch up with willingness?

There is no universal answer to that question. But there are useful ways to assess it.

Is the trajectory moving in the right direction, even if progress is slow? A partner who has fewer and less intense episodes this year compared to last year is showing neurobiological change, even if the episodes haven't stopped entirely.

Is your partner taking increasing responsibility for their own regulation? Early in recovery, they may need significant external support. Over time, they should be developing more independent capacity to manage their responses.

Is the repair process getting better? Even if ruptures still occur, is your partner able to re-engage more quickly, take accountability more readily, and participate in repair more effectively than before?

If the answers to these questions are consistently yes, the gap between willingness and capacity is likely closing. If the answers are consistently no, or if the trajectory has flatlined or reversed, that is important information.

Consider Elowen (name changed), whose partner had been in trauma therapy for three years. "The first year, I saw huge changes. The second year, things plateaued, and I got scared. My partner's therapist told us that plateaus are normal, that the brain needs time to consolidate gains before the next phase. And she was right. Year three brought a new wave of progress. But I had to trust the process, and honestly, there were months when that trust was almost gone."

Elowen's experience is instructive, but it also comes with a caveat. Trusting the process is reasonable when there is a process to trust: consistent treatment, visible effort, a qualified therapist, and measurable (even if slow) progress. Trusting the process when there is no process, when treatment is sporadic and accountability is absent, is not patience. It is wishful thinking.

Reflection prompt: Has the gap between your partner's willingness and their capacity been narrowing over the past year? What specific evidence do you have either way?

What Therapy Can Change

When CPTSD treatment is consistent, appropriate, and engaged with genuinely, research documents several areas of meaningful improvement.

Emotional regulation. One of the primary goals of CPTSD treatment is expanding the window of tolerance and developing the capacity to manage intense emotions without becoming overwhelmed or shutting down. Studies on CPTSD treatment outcomes consistently show improvements in emotional regulation as one of the earliest and most reliable gains (Cloitre et al., 2011).

Flashback intensity and frequency. With appropriate trauma processing (EMDR, CPT, or similar approaches), the intensity and frequency of emotional flashbacks typically decrease over time. The traumatic memories don't disappear, but they lose their ability to hijack the present moment with the same force (Shapiro, 2018).

Mentalization. This is the ability to see another person's perspective, to understand that your internal state is separate from theirs. People with CPTSD often struggle with mentalization, which is why your partner may misread your intentions so frequently. Therapy, particularly approaches like mentalization-based treatment, can improve this capacity (Bateman and Fonagy, 2016).

Distress tolerance. The ability to sit with discomfort without immediately reacting. This skill develops over the course of treatment and directly affects relationship dynamics, because a partner with higher distress tolerance is less likely to escalate during conflict.

Communication skills. Therapy can help your partner learn to express needs, manage conflict, and engage in difficult conversations without defaulting to old survival patterns. This is often one of the later gains, because it requires a foundation of emotional regulation and distress tolerance first.

Trust capacity. Over time, sustained therapeutic work can help rebuild the capacity for trust that was damaged by early relational trauma. This is a slow process, and it's often the last area to show significant improvement, but it does happen.

What Therapy Probably Won't Change

Equally important is being honest about what therapy cannot do.

Core personality traits that predate trauma. Your partner's fundamental temperament, their introversion or extroversion, their baseline energy level, their interests and values, are not products of CPTSD and will not change through trauma treatment. If you've been waiting for your partner to become a fundamentally different kind of person, that expectation may not be realistic.

Compatibility issues independent of CPTSD. Some relationship problems have nothing to do with trauma. Differences in values, life goals, sexual compatibility, parenting styles, or communication preferences may be present regardless of your partner's diagnosis. Therapy can help your partner manage their trauma responses, but it cannot create compatibility where none naturally resides.

Your partner's motivation. Therapy does not create willingness. A skilled therapist can work with existing motivation, but they cannot manufacture it. If your partner is not motivated to do the work, no amount of excellent treatment will produce lasting change.

The damage already done. This is the piece that partners often find hardest to accept. Even if your partner makes significant progress in recovery, the relationship damage that has accumulated over months or years doesn't automatically repair. Research on relationship repair after relational injuries shows that repair is possible but requires active, sustained effort from both partners and often benefits from couples therapy with a trauma-informed practitioner (Johnson, 2019).

Your own depletion. Your partner's recovery does not restore you. As we discussed in Chapter 1.0, the toll of living in a CPTSD-affected relationship is real and cumulative. Even if your partner improves dramatically, you may still be carrying exhaustion, grief, resentment, and your own secondary stress responses. Your healing is a separate process that requires its own attention and support.

Reflection prompt: Which of these "won't change" items are most relevant to your situation? How does acknowledging them affect your thinking?

The Partner's Paradox

You can't heal your partner. Their recovery is their work, done in therapy, with professional support, on their own timeline. And yet your response matters. The way you show up in the relationship, the boundaries you set, the patience you offer and the patience you withhold, all of these influence the environment in which recovery does or doesn't happen.

This is the paradox. You are not responsible for their healing, but you are not irrelevant to it either. And the tension between these two truths creates an exhausting balancing act.

"Waiting for them to get better" is not a relationship plan. It is a holding pattern. And holding patterns drain your resources without moving you toward any destination. If you're going to stay in this relationship during your partner's recovery, you need something more active than waiting. You need agreements about what treatment looks like, what accountability looks like, and what your own non-negotiable needs are. (Chapter 7.0 will cover this in detail.)

Creating conditions for change means setting boundaries that support recovery (e.g., "I expect you to maintain regular therapy") while also protecting your own wellbeing (e.g., "I will not continue to absorb verbal aggression during flashbacks without a plan to address it"). These two goals are not in conflict. In fact, as we covered in Chapter 2.0, clear boundaries improve outcomes for both partners.

But creating conditions for change is different from sacrificing yourself for their process. If staying in the relationship is costing you your health, your identity, and your ability to function, then the conditions you're creating are not healthy for either of you. A depleted partner cannot provide the stability that supports recovery. And you deserve a life that is more than a support structure for someone else's healing.

Consider Crispin (name changed), who found himself in exactly this paradox. "I wanted to be the partner who stuck it out. I wanted to support her recovery. But my therapist pointed out that I'd lost twenty pounds, I wasn't sleeping, and I'd developed an anxiety condition I'd never had before. She asked me: 'Who is going to support your recovery?' That question changed everything for me. Not because I immediately left, but because I started treating my own wellbeing as something that counted."

Reflection prompt: How has the balance between supporting your partner's recovery and protecting your own wellbeing shifted over time? Which direction is it currently leaning?

The Change Evidence Assessment

This reflection exercise asks you to look at concrete evidence rather than promises, intentions, or your own hopes. The goal is to assess, honestly, whether meaningful change has occurred over the past six to twelve months.

For each question, answer based on what you've observed, not what your partner has said they'll do.

Has your partner been in consistent treatment during this period? How many sessions have they attended? Have there been significant gaps?

Can you point to specific behaviours that have measurably improved? Not "they seem a little better" but "they used to shut down for two days after conflict, and now they can re-engage within hours."

Has the frequency or intensity of harmful behaviour decreased?

When your partner causes harm, is the repair process getting more effective?

Are you seeing effort between therapy sessions? Is your partner practicing skills, reading materials, or trying new approaches in daily life?

How does your partner respond when you raise concerns? With accountability, or with defensiveness and blame?

If someone who knew you both a year ago saw your relationship today, would they notice positive change?

Sit with your answers. If you see evidence of real, measurable change, that is meaningful data that can inform your decision. If you don't see that evidence, or if the changes have been promised but not delivered, that is equally meaningful data.

Neither set of answers tells you what to do. Both sets of answers tell you what you're working with.

Your Next Steps

CPTSD recovery is possible, real, and documented by research. It is also slow, non-linear, and dependent on your partner's sustained willingness to engage with treatment. Therapy can change emotional regulation, flashback intensity, mentalization, distress tolerance, communication, and trust capacity. It cannot change core personality traits, create motivation that isn't there, fix compatibility issues unrelated to trauma, undo existing relationship damage, or restore your own depleted wellbeing. The gap between willingness and capacity is real, and only time and consistent effort can close it. Your role in this process is to support conditions for change while protecting your own health, identity, and needs. "Waiting for them to get better" is not a plan. Clear expectations, measurable benchmarks, and honest assessment of evidence are what allow you to make informed decisions about your future. The chapters ahead will help you apply this understanding to the specific question of staying or leaving.

Chapter 5 Hearing Your Own Voice

There's a particular kind of silence that develops in partners of CPTSD survivors. It's not the silence of having nothing to say. It's the silence of having trained yourself, over months or years, to make your own inner world smaller so that your partner's inner world can take up more room. It happens gradually. You stop mentioning things that bother you because mentioning them leads to a crisis. You stop expressing needs because your needs seem trivial compared to their suffering. You stop trusting your own perceptions because you've been told, so many times, that you're misreading the situation.

This chapter is about that silence and what it's cost you. And it's about the slow, necessary work of finding your way back to your own voice, your own perspective, and your own authority over your own life.

How Partners Get Silenced

The erosion of self-trust in CPTSD relationships rarely happens through one dramatic event. It happens through hundreds of small moments where your perception is questioned, your emotional response is treated as the problem, or your needs are deferred because something more urgent is always happening with your partner.

There are several common mechanisms.

Being told your perceptions are wrong. You bring up something that bothered you, and your partner responds by reframing the situation until you're no longer sure what happened. "That's not what I said." "You're remembering it wrong." "That's not how it went." Over time, you stop trusting your own memory and interpretation of events. This isn't always intentional. In some cases, your partner genuinely perceives events differently because their trauma filters distort their experience. But the effect on you is the same regardless of intent: your confidence in your own reality erodes.

Having your emotions treated as less urgent. In a relationship where one person has a diagnosed condition, a subtle hierarchy of suffering can develop. Your bad day doesn't count as much because their bad day involves flashbacks and shame spirals. Your anxiety doesn't merit attention because their anxiety is diagnosable. Your grief about the relationship gets pushed aside because their grief about their childhood takes precedence. Over time, you internalize the message that your emotional life is secondary, and you stop bringing it forward.

Being cast as "the stable one." Partners of CPTSD survivors are often framed, by the relationship, by family, by therapists, as the anchor, the rock, the stable presence. And while that framing may feel like a compliment, it functions as a cage. If you're the stable one, you can't have a breakdown. You can't fall apart. You can't say "I can't handle this." Research on role strain in caregiving relationships shows that being assigned the role of the "strong" partner significantly increases psychological distress while simultaneously reducing the likelihood of seeking support (Revenson et al., 2005).

Developing your own fawn response. As we discussed in Chapter 2.0, the fawn response is a survival strategy in which a person manages threat by becoming excessively accommodating. If you've spent years in a relationship where conflict triggers your partner's trauma responses, you may have developed your own version of this. You automatically adjust, accommodate, smooth over, and suppress. You do this not because you're weak but because your nervous system has learned that this is the most effective way to prevent escalation.

The cost is that you lose contact with what you actually think, feel, and want.

The result of all these mechanisms is what might be called **identity erosion**. You look in the mirror and you're not entirely sure who is looking back. "Partner of someone with CPTSD" has become your primary identity, and the person you were before this relationship has grown dim.

Consider Bramwell (name changed), who described this experience: "My sister asked me what I wanted for my birthday, and I couldn't answer. Not because I was being humble. Because I genuinely didn't know. I'd spent so many years focused on what my partner needed, what would trigger her, what would keep the peace, that I'd completely lost track of my own preferences. I couldn't tell you my favourite restaurant anymore. I couldn't remember the last book I'd read for myself. That scared me more than any argument."

Reflection prompt: Can you identify a moment when you chose not to express something you felt or needed because you anticipated it would cause a problem? How often does that happen in an average week?

When Compassion Gets Weaponized

Your compassion is probably one of the things you value most about yourself. It's what drew you into this relationship. It's what kept you here through the difficult years. And it may be the very thing that's now keeping you stuck.

Compassion gets weaponized in CPTSD relationships from three directions.

From your partner. Not always intentionally. But when your understanding of their condition is used to deflect accountability ("you know I can't help it when I'm triggered"), to silence your needs ("can you not bring this up right now, I'm having a bad day"), or to guilt you into staying ("you're the only person who understands me, I'd fall apart without you"), your compassion has become a tool that works against you. The line between genuine vulnerability and emotional leverage can be very thin, and it's one that partners in CPTSD relationships are often poorly positioned to see clearly because their empathy bias runs so strong.

From the mental health community. Online forums, support groups, and even some therapists can inadvertently contribute to the silencing of partners. The narrative that says "if you really loved them, you'd be more patient" or "their behaviour is a trauma response, not a choice" is not wrong on its face. But when it's applied without acknowledgment of the partner's experience, it becomes a way of saying your suffering doesn't count. Research on caregiver burden in mental health contexts confirms that inadequate recognition of caregiver distress is a significant factor in caregiver burnout and mental health decline (Awad and Voruganti, 2008).

From yourself. This may be the most insidious form. You've internalized the belief that your needs, your limits, and your pain are less important because your partner has a diagnosis and you don't. You hold yourself to an impossible standard: infinite patience, zero needs, perfect boundaries, constant availability. When you fall short of that standard (which every human being would), you blame yourself rather than questioning the standard.

The impossible standard deserves particular attention. No one can be infinitely patient. No one can function without their own needs being met. No one can maintain perfect boundaries in an environment where boundaries are constantly tested. The expectation that you should be able to do all of this, simply because your partner has CPTSD, is not reasonable. And the guilt you feel for falling short of it is not evidence of your failure. It is evidence that the standard was never achievable.

Consider Quinlan (name changed), who attended a support group for partners. "I went looking for help and walked out feeling worse. Every time I tried to talk about how hard things were, someone would remind me of what my partner was going through. Like I didn't know. Like I hadn't been living inside it every day. I started to think that maybe I was the problem. Maybe I just wasn't compassionate enough. It took a long time, and a good therapist, to see that my compassion wasn't the issue. My self-abandonment was."

Reflection prompt: In what ways have you held yourself to an impossible standard in this relationship? Where did that standard come from?

Reclaiming What's Yours

Two things can be true at the same time. Your partner is suffering from the effects of something terrible that was done to them. And you are suffering from the effects of the relationship dynamics that their trauma creates. These two truths do not cancel each other out. They are both real, and they both deserve attention.

This may sound obvious, but for many partners, it's a radical statement. You've spent so long prioritizing your partner's experience that the idea of your own experience being equally valid feels almost transgressive. But there is a difference between empathy and **self-abandonment**, and that difference matters enormously.

Empathy means being able to understand and share another person's feelings. It is a relational skill and a genuine strength. Self-abandonment means consistently sacrificing your own needs, perceptions, and wellbeing in service of another person's needs, to the point where you lose contact with yourself. Empathy connects. Self-abandonment erases. Research on compassion fatigue makes clear that unsustainable levels of other-directed empathy without adequate self-care lead to measurable psychological and physical decline (Figley, 2002).

Reclaiming your perspective starts with reconnecting to what you want, need, feel, and believe, separate from your partner's narrative about the relationship. This is not selfish. It is the minimum requirement for being a whole person inside a relationship.

What do you want from your life? Not what do you want for your partner, or what do you want for the relationship. What do you want for yourself? What kind of daily experience do you want to wake up to? What relationships, activities, and goals matter to you independently of this partnership?

What do you need? Not what are you willing to settle for. What do you actually need to feel safe, respected, and whole in a relationship?

What do you feel? Not what should you feel given your partner's circumstances. What is your actual emotional experience right now, unfiltered and unedited?

These questions may be harder to answer than you expect. If you've been operating in self-abandonment mode for a long time, your own wants, needs, and feelings may have gone underground. That's normal. They haven't disappeared. They've just been waiting for you to ask.

Reflection prompt: Set a timer for ten minutes. Write freely about what you want from your life, with no reference to your partner or your relationship. What comes up?

Rebuilding Self Trust

If your perceptions have been questioned, your emotions have been deprioritized, and your reality has been reframed for long enough, rebuilding trust in yourself takes deliberate practice. It doesn't happen all at once. But it can happen, and the exercises below are a starting point.

Body-based check-ins. Your body often knows things your mind is still arguing with. Research on interoception (the ability to sense internal bodily signals) shows that body awareness is closely linked to emotional awareness and decision-making quality (Critchley and Garfinkel, 2017). Start a daily practice of pausing and asking: What am I feeling in my body right now? Where is the tension? What does my gut tell me about this situation? You don't have to act on these signals immediately. You just have to start listening.

The Before and After inventory. Take a sheet of paper and draw a line down the middle. On one side, write words and phrases that described you before this relationship. On the other side, write words and phrases that describe you now. The gap between those two columns is data. It tells you what has changed, and it gives you a map of what you might want to reclaim.

Journaling for reconnection. Regular journaling, even ten minutes a day, creates a private space where your voice can come out uncensored. Research on expressive writing (which we introduced in the Introduction) shows that the process of writing about difficult emotional experiences improves psychological wellbeing, even when the writing is never shared with anyone (Pennebaker and Smyth, 2016). Write about what happened today. Write about how you felt. Write about what you wanted to say but didn't. Let the page be the one place where your experience doesn't need to be managed or minimized.

Values clarification. What matters to you? Not in theory. In practice. What values do you want your life to reflect? Honesty? Connection? Adventure? Stability? Creativity? Write down your top five values, and then honestly assess how much your current life reflects them. The gap between your values and your daily reality is another form of information, similar to the breaking point data we discussed in Chapter 1.0.

The trusted mirror exercise. If there is someone in your life who knew you before this relationship (a longtime friend, a sibling, a parent), ask them a simple question: "What have you noticed about how I've changed?" Listen to their answer without defending, explaining, or contextualizing. Their outside perspective may reflect truths that are hard to see from the inside.

Consider Godric (name changed), who tried the trusted mirror exercise with his college roommate. "He didn't sugarcoat it. He said, 'You used to be the funniest person in every room. Now you apologize for everything. You check your phone constantly. You don't laugh the same way.' Hearing it from someone who'd known me for fifteen years hit different than all the self-reflection I'd been doing on my own. It made it real in a way I couldn't argue with."

Reflection prompt: If you tried the Before and After inventory right now, what would be the biggest difference between the two columns?

Your Inner Authority

Rebuilding your inner authority means learning to treat your own perceptions, feelings, and judgments as trustworthy again. Not infallible (nobody's perceptions are perfect) but worthy of being taken seriously, starting by you.

Here's a distinction that may help: there is a difference between being "too sensitive" and being accurately attuned to a harmful situation. Partners of CPTSD survivors are frequently told (or tell themselves) that they're overreacting, being too demanding, or expecting too much. In some cases, that self-correction is appropriate. In many cases, it's a conditioned response to an environment that has systematically taught you to doubt yourself.

The question to ask is not "am I too sensitive?" The question is "what am I sensing?" If what you're sensing is a consistent pattern of harm, emotional depletion, or the slow erasure of your identity, then your sensitivity is not the problem. Your sensitivity is doing exactly what it's supposed to do: alerting you that something is wrong.

Practice small acts of self-trust every day. Express a preference when asked where to eat. Voice a mild disagreement when you notice one. Set a small boundary and hold it. These are not dramatic gestures. They're recalibrations. Each one is a quiet statement that says: my perspective matters. My needs are legitimate. I am allowed to take up space.

And give yourself permission to have limits. You are allowed to have needs that don't bend around your partner's condition. You are allowed to have deal-breakers. You are allowed to look at your life and say "this is not working for me" without that statement being an act of cruelty toward someone you love.

As we move into Chapter 6.0, we'll look at the practical and emotional weight of shared history: children, finances, years together, and everything you've built. That weight is real. But it's best examined by a person who has reconnected with their own voice, their own values, and their own sense of what they need. This chapter is the foundation for that examination.

The Unsent Letter

This chapter's reflection exercise is a letter, one you write but do not send.

Write a letter to the version of yourself who first entered this relationship. Write it from where you stand now, with everything you now know and everything you've experienced since then.

You might tell that earlier version of yourself what's coming. You might thank them for their courage. You might grieve what they're about to lose. You might tell them what you wish they'd known.

This exercise isn't about regret. It's about perspective. The distance between who you were then and who you are now contains important information about what this relationship has cost you and what it has taught you. And writing it down, in your own words, to your own self, is an act of reclaiming your voice in its most direct form.

Take your time with it. There's no word count. There's no format. There's just you, speaking honestly, to the person who most deserves to hear it.

Key Takeaways

Partners of CPTSD survivors often experience a gradual silencing of their own voice through mechanisms including perception questioning, emotional deprioritization, role casting, and the development of their own adaptive fawn responses. Compassion can be weaponized from multiple directions: by the partner, by mental health communities, and by internalized impossible standards. Two truths coexist without cancelling each other: your partner's trauma is real, and your suffering from the relationship dynamics is also real. The difference between empathy and self-abandonment is the line between staying connected to another person and losing connection to yourself. Rebuilding self-trust is a deliberate practice that includes body-based awareness, journaling, values clarification, and seeking outside perspectives from trusted people. Your inner authority deserves to be restored, your perceptions are worth taking seriously, and giving yourself permission to have needs and limits is not cruelty. It is the minimum requirement for remaining a whole person inside any relationship.

Chapter 6 The Weight of Shared History

If love were the only thing holding a relationship together, the decision to stay or leave would be straightforward. You'd ask yourself: do I still love this person? And the answer, whatever it was, would point you in a direction. But relationships aren't held together by love alone. They're held together by mortgages and school districts, by shared bank accounts and holiday traditions, by the family who calls your partner their own, by the children who call both of you home.

This chapter is about the weight of all of that. Not to dismiss it and not to let it make the decision for you, but to look at it honestly. Some of what holds you in place is a genuine reason to stay. Some of it is fear dressed up as loyalty. And knowing which is which matters more than almost anything else in this process.

Children and the Hardest Question

If there are children involved, everything gets more complicated. Children are not a factor to weigh alongside the mortgage and the holiday schedule. They are the factor that changes the entire equation, and they deserve the honest, careful attention that most "should I stay" conversations rush past.

The first thing to acknowledge is that children absorb relational dynamics. Even when parents believe they're hiding their difficulties, research consistently shows that children are aware of emotional tension, conflict patterns, and parental distress at much younger ages than most adults assume. A meta-analysis of studies on interparental conflict found that children exposed to chronic, unresolved parental discord show elevated rates of anxiety, depression, behavioural problems, and difficulty with their own emotional regulation (Cummings and Davies, 2010). This is true even when the conflict is not loud or visible. Children sense the temperature of the house.

In CPTSD-affected households, what children absorb goes beyond ordinary marital tension. They may witness emotional dysregulation, unpredictable mood shifts, or a parent who periodically withdraws or becomes frightening. They may also absorb the other parent's hypervigilance, people-pleasing, and emotional suppression. In other words, they're learning both sides of the dynamic: how to be overwhelmed by emotions and how to disappear yourself to keep the peace.

The question "should I stay for the kids?" deserves an honest answer, and the honest answer is: it depends on what staying looks like. Research does not support the blanket claim that two-parent households are always better for children. What research does support is that stable, low-conflict households are better for children than high-conflict ones, regardless of whether one or two parents are present (Amato, 2010). If staying means the household remains chaotic, tense, and emotionally unpredictable, staying is not protecting your children. It is exposing them to the very dynamics you're trying to shield them from.

Co-parenting with a CPTSD partner after separation is genuinely difficult. Your partner may experience the separation as abandonment, which can trigger intense trauma responses. They may struggle with consistency, boundaries, and emotional regulation during handoffs and transitions. But co-parenting from separate households, with appropriate support and clear boundaries, is often less harmful to children than co-parenting from inside a relationship that is causing both parents measurable distress.

Consider Hadrian (name changed), who agonized over the impact on his two young children. "My therapist asked me to describe what my kids saw on a daily basis. Not the big blowups, just the regular stuff. And when I said it out loud (me tiptoeing around, their mom crying in the bedroom, the tension at dinner, the weekends where nobody talked), I could hear how bad it sounded. I'd been telling myself staying was better for them. But what I was really doing was raising them inside exactly the kind of environment I was trying to protect them from."

Reflection prompt: If your children could describe the emotional atmosphere of your home in their own words, what do you think they would say?

The Practical Anchors

Beyond children, there are tangible, material realities that make leaving complicated. These deserve honest acknowledgment because pretending they don't matter only adds confusion to an already difficult situation.

Financial entanglement. Shared mortgages, joint debts, combined incomes, one partner's financial dependency on the other. Separation has real financial consequences, and in many cases, both partners will experience a significant reduction in their standard of living after a split. This is not a reason to stay in an unsustainable relationship, but it is a reality that requires planning. Financial preparation (which we'll cover in more detail in Chapter 8.0) is a practical step, not a betrayal.

Housing. Where will you live? Where will your partner live? If you own a home together, what happens to it? These questions feel overwhelming, and their overwhelming nature is part of what keeps people in place. The logistical complexity of separation can function as a kind of paralysis: you can't figure out the housing, so you don't think about leaving, and because you're not thinking about leaving, you don't figure out the housing. Breaking this cycle requires taking one practical step at a time, and giving yourself permission to plan without committing to a final decision.

Extended relationships. In-laws who have become family. Shared friendships where the social fabric will tear if you separate. Community ties (religious communities, neighbourhood connections, school networks) where your identity as a couple is woven in. The loss of these connections is real grief, and it belongs on the list of things you're weighing.

Logistical overwhelm as a default. Many partners stay not because they've decided to stay, but because the logistics of leaving feel so vast that inaction becomes the path of least resistance. This is not a decision. It is avoidance wearing the mask of commitment. If you're staying because leaving feels too complicated, that information is worth examining honestly.

Reflection prompt: Which practical factors feel most overwhelming to you right now? Are any of them genuinely insurmountable, or do they feel insurmountable because you're thinking about all of them at once?

The Emotional Anchors

The practical anchors are at least visible and nameable. The emotional anchors are harder to see, but they're often heavier.

Shared history. "We've been through so much together." This is one of the most powerful emotional anchors, and it deserves respect. The years you've shared are real. The experiences you've survived together are real. The bond forged in difficulty is real. But shared history is a record of what happened. It is not, by itself, a prediction of what should happen next.

The good memories. You fell in love with this person for reasons. There was a version of your partner (or a version of the relationship) that made you feel alive, connected, and hopeful.

Those memories are not fiction. They happened. And holding
them alongside the difficult reality of your present creates a
particular kind of grief: mourning something that still
technically lives but doesn't look the way it used to.

Fear of being alone. This one runs deep. The fear of starting
over in your forties, fifties, or beyond. The fear that you won't
find love again. The fear of waking up in an empty apartment
and wondering if you made the worst mistake of your life.
Research on post-separation adjustment shows that while the
initial period is often intensely painful, most individuals report
improved wellbeing within one to two years of separation,
particularly when the relationship involved chronic conflict or
distress (Sbarra and Emery, 2005).

Grief for the imagined future. You had a picture of how your
life was going to go. Retirement together, grandchildren,
growing old with someone who knew you before your hair
changed colour. Letting go of that picture is its own form of
loss, separate from the loss of the actual relationship.

Guilt. For many partners, guilt is the heaviest anchor of all.
Guilt about leaving someone who is suffering. Guilt about
prioritizing your own needs. Guilt about what it will do to them.
We'll address guilt specifically in the next section, because it
deserves its own careful examination.

The caretaker identity. If you've spent years as the person who
manages, supports, and stabilizes, you may have built an identity
around being needed. The question "who am I if I'm not
needed?" is genuinely unsettling. Leaving the relationship means
leaving the role, and that role, exhausting as it is, may have
become the structure around which your sense of self is
organized.

Consider Elowen (name changed), who recognized this pattern
in herself. "I realized that part of me didn't want to leave because

I didn't know who I'd be without the caregiving. Being the person who held everything together gave me a purpose. A terrible, exhausting, soul-crushing purpose, but a purpose. My therapist helped me see that I was afraid of the emptiness. Not the emptiness of being without my partner, but the emptiness of being without a crisis to manage."

Reflection prompt: Which emotional anchor weighs heaviest for you? What would it feel like to set it down, even temporarily?

The Sunk Cost Trap

The **sunk cost fallacy** is a well-documented cognitive bias in which people continue investing in something (a project, a relationship, a course of action) because of the resources already spent, rather than because the future return justifies further investment. In economics, this is considered irrational because past costs are unrecoverable regardless of future decisions (Arkes and Blumer, 1985).

In relationships, the sunk cost fallacy sounds like: "I've given this person twelve years. I can't just throw that away." Or: "We've been through so much. It would be a waste to leave now." Or: "I've invested everything I have in making this work."

Here's what needs to be said clearly: the years you've already given are gone regardless of what you decide next. Staying another year doesn't honour those twelve years. It just adds a thirteenth. The question is not "what have I already invested?" The question is "what do I want the next year of my life to look like?"

This doesn't mean those years were wasted. They were lived. They contained real love, real learning, real growth. They brought you children, or memories, or insights about yourself that you wouldn't have gained any other way. Honouring your history means carrying what it taught you forward. It does not mean remaining in a situation that is no longer sustainable because leaving would feel like admitting the investment didn't pay off.

The difference between honouring your history and being held hostage by it comes down to this: honouring means acknowledging what was, with gratitude and grief. Being held hostage means using what was to justify what shouldn't continue.

Reflection prompt: If you removed the years you've already invested from the equation and looked only at the relationship as it stands today, what would you see?

Separating Guilt from Love

Guilt is not love. Obligation is not love. Fear of what will happen to your partner without you is not love. These emotions often feel like love, because they involve the same person and carry the same intensity. But they operate differently, and confusing them with love can keep you trapped in a situation that love alone would not sustain.

The question "what will happen to them if I leave?" is one that almost every partner in this situation asks. And it's worth examining honestly.

Your partner is an adult. They have agency, even if CPTSD complicates that agency. They have (or can access) professional support. They have their own capacity for resilience, even if that capacity has been diminished by their trauma history. The belief that your partner cannot survive without you may feel like compassion, but it also contains an assumption that is worth questioning: that they are fundamentally incapable of managing their own life. For most partners with CPTSD, this assumption is not accurate. It is a story that has been reinforced by the caregiving dynamic but does not reflect their actual capacity (Tedeschi and Calhoun, 2004).

The guilt of leaving someone who is "sick" deserves particular attention. The framing of CPTSD as an illness creates a powerful guilt trap: you don't leave someone who is sick. But CPTSD is not a terminal illness that requires a bedside vigil. It is a condition that responds to treatment, that your partner has agency over (in terms of seeking and engaging with that treatment), and that does not obligate you to sacrifice your own wellbeing indefinitely. You can care about someone deeply and still recognize that the relationship is not something you can sustain.

Compassionate honesty means saying: "I love you. I am not able to stay. Both of those things are true."

Consider Dunstan (name changed), who spent two years wrestling with guilt before making his decision. "The guilt nearly destroyed me. I felt like I was abandoning a wounded person. But my therapist pointed out something that changed my thinking. She said, 'You're not the only person in the world who can support him. You're just the person who's been doing it. And you're allowed to stop.' That didn't make the guilt disappear. But it made it smaller. Small enough that I could think clearly around it."

Reflection prompt: If you're honest with yourself, how much of what holds you in this relationship is love, and how much is guilt or obligation?

What You're Actually Weighing

This is not a simple comparison of advantages and disadvantages. The decision you're facing is more like a question about identity and direction: what kind of life do you want to live, and is that life possible within this relationship as it currently functions?

That question requires you to factor in something that partners of CPTSD survivors often forget to include: your own happiness, health, and future. Not as a bonus or an afterthought, but as a legitimate, central consideration. You are allowed to want a life that doesn't revolve around managing someone else's condition. You are allowed to want peace, stability, and the freedom to be yourself without monitoring every word. You are allowed to factor your own wellbeing into this decision with the same weight you give to everyone else's.

Honouring the weight of what you've built means taking it seriously. It means not making impulsive decisions and not dismissing the real costs of leaving. But honouring the weight does not mean letting it pin you to the ground. You can respect what you've built and still decide that the foundation isn't supporting the life you need.

The Weight Inventory

This reflection exercise asks you to get everything out of your head and onto paper. The goal is clarity, not a verdict.

Make two columns. In the first column, list every factor that holds you in this relationship. Be specific. Include practical factors (mortgage, children's school, shared finances), emotional factors (love, guilt, fear of being alone, grief), relational factors (in-laws, friends, community), and any others that come to mind.

In the second column, next to each factor, write one of two labels: "reason to stay" or "reason I'm afraid to leave."

A reason to stay is something that genuinely adds to your life and would be meaningfully lost. A reason you're afraid to leave is something that keeps you in place through fear, guilt, or inertia rather than through genuine value.

Some items may be both. That's fine. Mark them as both.

Now look at your list. How many genuine reasons to stay do you have? How many fear-based anchors? The ratio between those two categories is information, the kind of information that, as we discussed in Chapter 1.0, deserves to be taken seriously rather than argued away.

Carry this inventory with you as you move into the next two chapters. Chapter 7.0 will show you what staying could look like if you decide to stay differently. Chapter 8.0 will show you what leaving could look like if you decide to go carefully. Both paths require the honesty you've practiced here.

The Bottom Line

The weight of shared history is real, and this chapter has taken it seriously. Children, finances, housing, extended relationships, shared memories, fear, guilt, and identity are all legitimate factors in your decision. But factors and reasons are not the same thing. Some of what holds you in place is a genuine reason to stay. Some of it is fear, guilt, or the sunk cost fallacy keeping you locked in a situation that no longer serves either of you. The difference between honouring your history and being trapped by it is the willingness to look at each factor honestly and ask: is this pulling me toward something I want, or holding me in something I've outgrown? Your happiness, health, and future deserve to be weighted as heavily as every other consideration on the list. They are not selfish additions. They are the centre of the equation.

Chapter 7 Staying Done Differently

If you've read the previous chapters and you're leaning toward staying, this chapter is for you. But it comes with a condition: staying the same way is not an option. If nothing changes about how this relationship operates, the dynamics that brought you to this book will bring you back to it. Or they'll bring you to a breaking point that doesn't allow for a thoughtful decision at all.

Staying is only meaningful if it comes with structural change. Not just promises, not just renewed effort for a few weeks after a crisis, but genuine, measurable shifts in how the relationship functions. This chapter lays out what that looks like: the conversations that need to happen, the professional support that needs to be in place, the agreements that need to be made, and the self-protection you need to maintain throughout.

This is not about saving the relationship through sheer willpower. It's about building a different kind of relationship with the same person, one where both partners have what they need to function and where the CPTSD dynamics are managed rather than endured.

Staying as an Active Choice

The decision to stay needs to be exactly that: a decision. Not a default. Not the path of least resistance. Not the thing you do because leaving feels too hard. An active, conscious, ongoing choice that you make with clarity about what you're choosing and what it will require.

What does intentional staying look like?

It means both partners acknowledge that the current dynamic is unsustainable. Not just you. Your partner also needs to see clearly that the way things have been operating is causing harm to both of you. If your partner believes everything is fine, or that you're the only one with a problem, intentional staying becomes impossible because you're trying to restructure a relationship that only one person agrees needs restructuring.

It means committing to specific changes, not general aspirations. "I'll try harder" is not a plan. "I will attend weekly therapy, use the crisis plan we create together when I'm triggered, and participate in monthly relationship check-ins" is a plan. The difference between intention and structure is the difference between hope and actual change.

It means accepting that staying is not a one-time decision. It is something you'll revisit, reassess, and recommit to (or not) on an ongoing basis. You are allowed to decide today that you're staying and decide in six months that you've changed your mind. Staying is not a life sentence. It is a choice you make for as long as the conditions that support it remain in place.

Consider Aldwyn (name changed), who described making this shift. "For years, I was staying by default. I wasn't choosing to be there. I was just failing to leave. When my therapist helped me reframe it as an active choice, it changed everything. Suddenly I had conditions. I had expectations. I had a timeline. And my partner could either meet those conditions or she couldn't, but at least we both knew what the deal was."

Reflection prompt: Are you currently staying as an active choice, or staying by default? What would need to change for it to become a genuine decision?

Restructuring the Relationship

Most CPTSD-affected relationships develop an unspoken structure over time: one partner carries the emotional weight, manages the triggers, absorbs the dysregulation, and keeps the household running. The other partner is cast (often unwillingly) in the role of the person who needs to be managed. Neither role is healthy, and neither partner thrives in it.

Restructuring means moving from a caretaker-patient dynamic to a partnership. This doesn't happen overnight, and it doesn't happen without friction. But it's the only configuration that allows both people to maintain their dignity and their health.

Redistributing emotional labour. If you've been the person who monitors moods, manages triggers, mediates with family, handles logistics during crises, and provides the emotional processing for the entire household, that labour needs to be named and redistributed. Research on emotional labour in intimate relationships shows that unequal distribution is a consistent predictor of relationship dissatisfaction and partner burnout (Erickson, 2005). Your partner may not be able to carry an equal share immediately, but the trajectory needs to move toward balance.

Creating explicit agreements. Unspoken rules are the enemy of sustainable relationships. What are the expectations around trigger management? Who does what during a crisis? What behaviours are acceptable during dysregulation and what behaviours are not, regardless of the emotional state driving them? Making these agreements explicit removes ambiguity and gives both partners a shared reference point. Written agreements may feel unromantic, but they are far more effective than unspoken hopes.

Structured communication. Regularly scheduled check-ins (weekly or biweekly) where both partners discuss what's working, what isn't, and what needs to change. Agreed-upon time-out protocols during conflict (not stonewalling, but mutually agreed pauses with a specific plan to return to the conversation). Repair rituals after ruptures: what does genuine repair look like in your relationship, and is it happening consistently? Research by John Gottman and colleagues found that the ability to repair after conflict is a stronger predictor of relationship success than the absence of conflict itself (Gottman and Silver, 2015).

The non-negotiables. What must be in place for you to stay? Not what would be nice. What is essential. This list is yours to write, and it should be honest. Common non-negotiables for partners in CPTSD-affected relationships include: consistent engagement with individual therapy, no physical aggression under any circumstances, willingness to participate in couples therapy, and a demonstrated effort to take accountability after harmful behaviour.

Reflection prompt: What are your three to five non-negotiables? If you told your partner about them tomorrow, how do you think they would respond?

Getting the Right Help

If you're going to stay, professional support is not optional for either of you.

Individual therapy for your partner is the foundation. Without it, recovery doesn't happen. As we covered in Chapter 4.0, CPTSD responds to evidence-based trauma treatment (EMDR, CPT, IFS, somatic experiencing, schema therapy), but that treatment needs to be consistent and ongoing. If your partner is not in individual therapy, or is attending sporadically, this is the first thing that needs to change.

Individual therapy for you is equally non-negotiable. You have been living inside a high-stress relational dynamic for an extended period, and as we discussed in Chapters 1.0 and 5.0, the toll on you is real and cumulative. You need a space where your experience is the priority, where you can process your own emotions without managing your partner's at the same time, and where a professional can help you rebuild the self-trust and clarity that may have eroded.

Couples therapy can be enormously helpful, but it comes with an important caveat. Standard couples therapy is designed for relationships where both partners have relatively equal power and a basic level of emotional safety. In relationships involving active abuse or severe power imbalances, couples therapy can inadvertently give the harmful partner new tools for manipulation or put the other partner at risk. The key is finding a **trauma-informed couples therapist** who understands CPTSD dynamics, can assess for safety, and can work with the specific patterns that trauma creates in relationships. Emotionally Focused Therapy (EFT), adapted for trauma, has shown particular promise for couples where one partner has a trauma history (Johnson, 2019).

Finding the right therapist matters more than most people realize. What to look for: specific training in trauma (not just general therapy licensure), experience working with CPTSD (not just single-incident PTSD), and a willingness to hear both partners' perspectives without defaulting to the position that the traumatized partner's experience is the only one that matters. Red flags in practitioners: dismissing the non-traumatized partner's experience, pressuring you to "be more patient," or failing to hold the CPTSD partner accountable for the impact of their behaviour.

Support groups for partners can also provide community and validation. Hearing from others who understand your specific situation, without having to explain the basics, can reduce isolation significantly.

Reflection prompt: What professional support is currently in place for your relationship? What's missing?

New Agreements for a Different Relationship

The Relationship Reset Conversation is one of the most difficult and most important conversations you'll have. It's the moment where you lay out, clearly and compassionately, what needs to change for you to stay. Here's how to approach it.

Timing matters. Don't have this conversation during or immediately after a crisis. Choose a time when both partners are relatively calm, rested, and not in an activated emotional state. If that window never seems to open, that itself is information worth noting.

Be specific. Not "I need things to get better" but "I need you to attend therapy weekly, I need us to have a crisis plan for when you're triggered, and I need us to check in on how we're doing every two weeks." Specific requests can be responded to. Vague hopes cannot.

Acknowledge the difficulty. Your partner is being asked to make changes while managing a condition that makes change harder than it would be for someone without CPTSD. That's real. Acknowledging it is not the same as excusing inaction, but it does show that you see the full picture.

Written agreements may feel clinical, but they work. A simple document that outlines what both partners have agreed to, what the expectations are, and what happens if those expectations aren't met gives both of you something concrete to return to. It also prevents the common dynamic where agreements are made in a moment of emotional intensity and then slowly eroded as daily life takes over.

Crisis plans deserve particular attention. What happens when your partner is triggered? What is their responsibility in that moment (using grounding techniques, calling their therapist, asking for space) and what is yours (giving space without pursuing, not taking the bait during a shame storm, activating your own self-care plan)? What happens when you're at your limit? Having these plans in writing, agreed upon during a calm moment, makes them far more likely to be followed during the chaos of an actual crisis.

Escalation protocols address what happens when things go beyond what the crisis plan can handle. When is it appropriate to call a therapist for an emergency session? When does one partner need to leave the house temporarily? When is professional crisis intervention needed? Having these steps mapped out in advance removes the paralyzing "what do I do?" from the worst moments.

Regular reviews keep the agreements alive. A quarterly check-in where both partners honestly assess how the agreements are working, what needs to be adjusted, and whether the relationship is moving in the direction both people agreed on. Without these reviews, agreements decay. With them, both partners have scheduled opportunities to raise concerns before they become crises.

Reflection prompt: If you were to draft a crisis plan for your relationship right now, what would be on it?

Protecting Yourself While Staying

Staying does not mean dissolving your boundaries. It means holding them more clearly than ever.

Boundaries that preserve you. You are allowed to say: "I will not continue this conversation while you are yelling." You are allowed to say: "I need to leave the room when things escalate, and I will come back when we can talk calmly." You are allowed to say: "I love you and I am not able to absorb this right now." Boundaries are not punishments. They are the structures that make continued closeness possible. Research consistently shows that clear interpersonal boundaries improve relationship satisfaction and reduce caregiver distress (Henry et al., 2011).

Maintaining your own life. Friendships that aren't connected to your partner. Hobbies and activities that are yours alone. Time that belongs to you. As we covered in Chapter 5.0, the erosion of identity is one of the most damaging effects of living in a CPTSD-affected relationship. Actively maintaining your own life is not abandoning your partner. It is preserving the person your partner fell in love with, and it is protecting your ability to show up as a whole person in the relationship.

Financial awareness. Even within a committed relationship, you benefit from maintaining financial literacy and some degree of financial independence. Know where the money is. Have access to accounts. Understand your financial picture. This is not about preparing to leave. It is about maintaining adult agency within any relationship.

An internal timeline. Give yourself a private, honest assessment of how long you're willing to invest in this restructured approach. Not an ultimatum to deliver to your partner, but an internal framework that keeps you from drifting indefinitely. "I am going to give this restructured relationship twelve months of genuine effort, and then I will reassess honestly." That kind of internal clarity prevents the slow slide back into indefinite waiting.

Permission to change your mind. Perhaps most importantly: staying today does not obligate you to stay tomorrow. If the conditions you've set are not met, if the agreements are broken, if the dynamic reverts to what it was before, you are allowed to reconsider. Staying is a renewable commitment, not a permanent contract. You can love someone and still reach the honest conclusion that the relationship is not going to work. That conclusion is available to you at any point, and reaching it does not undo the genuine effort you made.

Consider Fenwick (name changed), who stayed with his partner under a restructured agreement. "We wrote everything down. Therapy schedules, crisis protocols, monthly check-ins. It felt strange at first, like we were treating our relationship like a business plan. But honestly, it was the first time in years that I felt like we were both accountable. And when things got hard, we had something to go back to. Not just feelings, but agreements. That made all the difference."

The Conditions for Staying

This reflection exercise asks you to draft your personal list of conditions. Not hopes. Not wishes. Conditions: the things that need to be true for you to stay in this relationship sustainably.

Write down everything that needs to be in place. Think about therapy, accountability, behaviour changes, communication patterns, treatment of you during crises, and any other factors specific to your situation.

Now go through the list and honestly assess: how many of these conditions are currently being met?

For the conditions that aren't being met, ask: is my partner willing and able to work toward meeting them? What evidence supports my answer?

Is there a timeline that feels reasonable for these conditions to be met?

What will I do if, after genuine effort, the conditions remain unmet?

This is not an exercise in pessimism. It is an exercise in clarity. If the conditions can be met and both partners are willing to work toward them, staying has a real foundation. If the conditions are unrealistic, or if your partner is unable or unwilling to work toward them, that is equally important to know. The chapters ahead (and this book as a whole) support whatever conclusion your honest assessment leads you to.

Moving Forward

Staying in a CPTSD-affected relationship can work, but only if both partners commit to making it a different relationship than the one that brought you to crisis. This means restructuring the dynamic from caretaker-patient to partnership, getting professional support for both individuals and the relationship, creating explicit and written agreements about expectations and crisis management, and maintaining your own identity, boundaries, and self-care throughout the process. Staying is not a one-time decision but an ongoing, renewable choice that you make for as long as the conditions you've set remain in place. You are allowed to set non-negotiable requirements. You are allowed to maintain an internal timeline. And you are allowed to change your mind if the evidence tells you that the restructured approach isn't working. What you're building here is not a perfect relationship. It's a sustainable one. And sustainability requires honesty from both partners about what they can offer, what they need, and what they're willing to work toward.

Chapter 8 Leaving Done Carefully

If you've read the previous chapters and you're leaning toward leaving, this chapter is for you. And if reading that sentence brought up a wave of guilt, dread, or fear, that's expected. Leaving a partner with CPTSD is one of the most emotionally complicated decisions a person can make, and the complexity doesn't dissolve just because the decision feels right.

This chapter is about how to leave well. Not painlessly (that isn't possible) but with integrity, care, and sufficient planning to protect both of you as much as the situation allows. You can end a relationship with someone you still love. You can prioritize your own life without being cruel. You can walk away from something unsustainable and still carry compassion for the person you're leaving behind.

What you cannot do is leave perfectly. There is no version of this that doesn't hurt. But there are versions that cause less damage than others, and this chapter aims to help you find one of them.

You Are Not Abandoning Anyone

The narrative that leaving a CPTSD partner constitutes abandonment is powerful, and it may be the single biggest obstacle between you and a clear decision. So this needs to be addressed directly.

You are not abandoning a helpless person. You are making a decision about your own life. Your partner is an adult with agency, with the capacity to seek support, and with a trauma history that is their responsibility to address, not yours to absorb indefinitely. Leaving is not proof that you didn't try hard enough. If you've read this far, you've almost certainly tried harder than most people would.

There is a difference between leaving cruelly and leaving honestly. Leaving cruelly means disappearing without explanation, using the departure as punishment, attacking your partner's character on the way out, or deliberately timing the departure to cause maximum pain. Leaving honestly means being direct about your reasons, being compassionate in your delivery, and being responsible in your planning, while still holding firm to the decision itself.

Your partner's CPTSD does not obligate you to stay. As we discussed in Chapter 6.0, the framing of CPTSD as an illness that requires your permanent caregiving is a trap. Your partner needs professional support. That support is not you. And their recovery, if it happens, will happen through their own work with trained professionals, not through your continued self-sacrifice.

Consider Ivor (name changed), who struggled with this framing for years. "I kept thinking: what kind of person leaves someone who's been through what she's been through? It took a long time for my therapist to help me see that the question was rigged. It assumed that staying was the only moral option and that leaving was always wrong. But my staying wasn't helping her. It was enabling a dynamic where neither of us was getting what we needed."

Reflection prompt: What story have you been telling yourself about what leaving would say about you as a person? Is that story accurate, or is it a guilt narrative?

Preparing to Leave

Leaving a CPTSD-affected relationship requires more preparation than a typical separation. Your partner's trauma means that the departure itself can trigger intense responses:

abandonment terror, shame spirals, desperate attempts to reconnect, or in some cases, escalation to threats or harm. Planning ahead is not manipulative. It is responsible.

Safety planning. If there is any risk of escalation (verbal or physical), develop a safety plan before initiating the conversation. This includes: identifying where you will go if you need to leave quickly, having important documents (identification, financial records, custody documents) in a secure location, alerting a trusted friend or family member about your plan and timeline, and having the number of a domestic violence hotline accessible. If your situation involves any of the red lines we discussed in Chapter 3.0 (physical violence, threats, coercive control), professional safety planning with a domestic violence advocate is essential.

Financial preparation. Before announcing your decision, make sure you understand your financial picture. This includes: knowing the balances of all joint accounts, understanding your individual credit situation, having access to funds that will cover immediate needs (first month's rent, deposits, basic expenses), and gathering any financial documents you may need for legal proceedings. If your partner controls the finances, this preparation may need to happen discreetly, and a domestic violence advocate can help you develop a plan.

Housing. Where will you live? Where will your partner live? If you own a home together, which of you will remain in it during the separation process? These questions need at least preliminary answers before you initiate the conversation. You don't need every detail figured out, but you need enough of a plan that the logistics don't become a reason to reverse your decision in the first difficult days.

Legal considerations. If you're married, or if children are involved, consult a family law attorney before initiating the separation if at all possible. Understanding your rights, obligations, and options regarding custody, property, and support gives you a foundation of knowledge that protects both you and your children. Many attorneys offer initial consultations at reduced rates.

Building your support network. Identify the people who will be in your corner during this process. A therapist, a trusted friend, a family member who understands the situation. You will need people who can listen without judgment, provide practical help, and remind you of your reasons when guilt tries to pull you back. Research on social support during relationship dissolution consistently shows that having even one or two reliable support people significantly improves adjustment outcomes (Cohen and Wills, 1985).

Timing. There is never a "good time" to leave. But there are safer times. Avoid initiating the conversation during a crisis, immediately after a flashback or shame storm, or when your partner is already in an acutely vulnerable state. Choose a time when both of you are relatively stable, when you have support available afterward, and when you have somewhere to go if the conversation becomes unmanageable.

Reflection prompt: What practical steps do you still need to take before you're ready to have the conversation?

Having the Conversation

How you tell a CPTSD partner that you're leaving matters. It matters for their wellbeing, for yours, and for any ongoing co-parenting relationship. Here's how to approach it.

Be direct. Don't hint. Don't "start a discussion." Don't frame it as "I've been thinking about whether maybe we should consider..." If you've made the decision, say so clearly. "I've made the decision to end our relationship." The clarity, while painful, is more respectful than ambiguity, which gives false hope and prolongs suffering for both of you.

Be compassionate but firm. You can acknowledge your partner's pain without reversing your decision. "I know this is devastating, and I'm sorry for the pain this causes. I care about you deeply, and I'm not able to continue in this relationship." These are not contradictory statements. They are honest ones.

Don't catalogue their failures. This is not the time for a comprehensive list of everything they've done wrong. If they ask why, keep it honest but general: "The dynamic between us has been unsustainable for me, and I don't believe it can change enough for me to stay." You don't owe them a detailed indictment, and providing one will only deepen the wound without serving any constructive purpose.

Manage their reaction without abandoning your decision. Your partner may cry, rage, plead, threaten, shut down, or dissociate. These responses are understandable given their trauma history. You can sit with their pain for a reasonable period without changing your mind. But if the conversation becomes unsafe, or if you feel your resolve weakening under the pressure of their distress, you are allowed to end the conversation and return to it later. "I can see this is extremely painful. I'm going to give you some space right now, and we can talk about the practical next steps when you're ready."

The abandonment framing. Your partner may frame your departure as another abandonment, another betrayal, another person who left. This is understandable. From inside their trauma history, that is genuinely how it may feel. But their interpretation of your decision is not the same as the reality of your decision. You are not their childhood caregiver who left. You are an adult who made a considered choice after sustained effort. You can acknowledge their pain ("I understand that this connects to deep wounds for you") without accepting responsibility for their entire history of loss.

When not to have the conversation. In situations involving physical violence, escalating threats, or coercive control, you may need to leave without a face-to-face conversation. Your safety takes precedence over a "proper" departure. A letter, a message through a therapist, or a conversation facilitated by a professional are all legitimate alternatives when direct conversation poses a risk. This is not cowardice. It is self-preservation.

Reflection prompt: If you were going to have this conversation tomorrow, what would you say? Write it out. Let yourself see the words.

The Guilt After

The guilt will come. It will come when you see their name on your phone. It will come when mutual friends ask how they're doing. It will come at three in the morning when you lie in the dark and wonder if you've made a terrible mistake. And the guilt doesn't mean you're wrong.

Guilt after leaving a CPTSD partner is nearly universal among caring, empathic people. That's what you are. The same qualities that made you a devoted partner (your empathy, your compassion, your capacity for loyalty) will now generate guilt as a byproduct of the decision to leave. Knowing this in advance doesn't eliminate the guilt, but it helps you recognize it for what it is: a feeling, not a verdict.

Common guilt narratives and how to respond to them:

"What if they can't cope without me?" They managed before you. They can manage after you. And the support they need is professional, not romantic. If they are in genuine crisis, connecting them with a therapist, a crisis line, or a trusted friend is appropriate. Staying in an unsustainable relationship out of fear for their coping is not appropriate, and research on codependent caregiving patterns confirms that this dynamic serves neither partner's long-term wellbeing (Dear et al., 2005).

"I should have tried harder." You tried. You researched their condition, adjusted your life around their needs, absorbed their pain, and lost parts of yourself in the process. The question is not whether you tried hard enough. The question is whether trying harder would produce a different outcome.

"Everyone will judge me for leaving someone who's sick." Some people will. Their opinions, however well-intentioned, are not data about the quality of your decision. The people who know you and who understand the full picture are the only opinions that matter, and most of them are probably relieved you're prioritizing yourself.

Guilt versus grief. These two feelings are often confused. Guilt says: "I did something wrong." Grief says: "I lost something I valued." Much of what you're experiencing is grief, and grief is appropriate. You are losing a partner, a shared future, a version of your life. Allow yourself to grieve without translating that grief into evidence that you made the wrong choice.

The guilt of relief. When leaving feels like the first full breath you've taken in years, the relief itself can trigger guilt. How can I feel better when they're in so much pain? The answer is: because you've been in pain too, and your nervous system is finally beginning to register its own release. Relief is not cruelty. It is your body telling you what it needed.

Consider Jory (name changed), who described the aftermath of his decision. "The first two weeks were terrible. Guilt like I'd never felt. But by the third week, I noticed something. I was sleeping through the night for the first time in years. I wasn't scanning for mood shifts when I came home. My shoulders weren't up around my ears. And as much as I felt guilty about feeling better, the fact that I felt so much better so quickly told me something important about how bad things had been."

Reflection prompt: What do you think the first week after leaving would actually feel like? Not what you fear it would feel like, but what you honestly think would happen?

What the First Months Look Like

The emotional reality of the first days, weeks, and months after leaving is non-linear and often confusing.

The first days are usually the hardest. Adrenaline, grief, guilt, and disorientation combine to create a state that feels like an emergency. This is temporary, even though it doesn't feel temporary while you're in it.

The first weeks may bring waves of doubt. "Did I make a mistake?" is a nearly universal question during this period. Research on post-separation adjustment suggests that doubt is a normal part of the process and does not, by itself, indicate that the decision was wrong (Sbarra and Emery, 2005). The urge to go back is often strongest during this phase, and it's worth examining honestly whether that urge comes from genuine reassessment or from the discomfort of change.

The first months are where the adjustment begins in earnest. You start rebuilding routines. The acute grief begins to settle into something more manageable. You may notice improvements in your physical health, your sleep, your mood. You may also experience unexpected grief, missing things you didn't expect to miss.

The temptation to go back deserves specific attention. Many partners return to CPTSD-affected relationships, sometimes multiple times. This isn't necessarily wrong, but it requires honest assessment. Are you going back because genuine change has occurred? Or are you going back because the pain of separation is intense and returning is the fastest way to make it stop? Research on on-again, off-again relationships shows that cycling between separation and reunion is associated with lower relationship satisfaction and higher psychological distress than either stable togetherness or a clean break (Dailey et al., 2009).

Co-parenting after separation is its own chapter-length topic, but the essentials are these: maintain clear boundaries, communicate about the children only (not about the relationship), use a structured co-parenting tool or app if direct communication is too volatile, and involve a family therapist if the transition is rocky. Your children need consistency from both parents, and that consistency is easier to provide from a calm, separate household than from an unstable shared one.

Post-separation contact requires a conscious decision. How much contact is appropriate? For co-parents, some contact is necessary and should be limited to child-related matters. For partners without children, reducing or eliminating contact for a defined period often supports healthier adjustment for both people. If your partner pushes for contact beyond what you've agreed to, holding your boundary is an act of care, for you and for them. Maintaining a pseudo-relationship through ongoing contact delays both partners' healing.

Reflection prompt: What boundaries around post-separation contact would you need to set? What would be hardest about holding them?

Rebuilding After

The strange thing about leaving a relationship defined by crisis is the silence that follows. For the first time in possibly years, nobody needs you to manage anything. Nobody's mood requires your attention. The house is quiet, and the quiet can feel unsettling, because your nervous system became accustomed to running on alert.

This adjustment is normal. Research on post-caregiving adjustment shows that people who leave high-intensity caregiving roles often experience a period of disorientation, sometimes called "caregiver withdrawal," before their systems recalibrate to a lower-stress baseline (Schulz et al., 2004).

Rediscovering yourself is the work of this period. The exercises from Chapter 5.0 (the Before and After inventory, values clarification, body-based check-ins) are relevant again here, now with the added space to actually act on what they reveal. What did you used to love doing? Who were you before this relationship reshaped you? What do you want now?

Processing your own experience. You may have your own trauma from this relationship. Secondary traumatic stress, as we discussed in Chapter 1.0, can leave lasting marks. You may find yourself triggered by things that remind you of the old dynamic: a certain tone of voice, a particular look on someone's face, the sound of a door opening with too much force. Working through this with a therapist who understands relational trauma is important. You deserve the same quality of healing that you hoped your partner would pursue.

When to date again. There is no universal timeline, but there are signs of readiness: you can think about the past relationship without intense guilt or grief, you've done enough work on your own patterns to avoid repeating them, and you genuinely want connection rather than distraction. Many therapists suggest a minimum of six months to a year after a significant relationship before beginning a new one, but the actual timeline depends on your individual healing process.

The long view. Years from now, you will look back on this decision with the benefit of perspective. You'll see things you couldn't see from inside the relationship. You'll understand your own patterns more clearly. And whatever happens, the experience will have taught you something about your capacity for love, for endurance, and for the ultimately necessary act of choosing yourself.

Consider Larkin (name changed), who reflected on his departure two years later. "The first year was hell. Guilt, grief, doubt, all of it. But the second year, something shifted. I started remembering who I was. I started laughing differently. I started doing things because I wanted to, not because I was managing someone else's crisis. And when I looked back at the relationship, I could finally see it clearly. I didn't leave because I was weak. I left because I was honest."

The Compassionate Exit Plan

This chapter's reflection exercise is a structured planning tool. It isn't designed to push you out the door. It's designed to ensure that if you go, you go with your eyes open and your heart intact.

Practical preparation. List the practical steps you need to take before initiating the separation. Include financial, housing, legal, and logistical items. Note which ones are complete and which still need attention.

Support structure. Who will be your support during this process? List names and roles: therapist, trusted friend, family member, legal advisor. If any of these supports are missing, how will you put them in place?

The conversation. Write a draft of what you want to say. Keep it honest, compassionate, and firm. Include what you will do if the conversation becomes unsafe.

Self-compassion checkpoint. Write a short note to yourself that you can return to when the guilt hits hardest. Include: why you made this decision, what you tried before arriving here, and what you need to remember about your own right to a sustainable life.

The first week plan. Where will you be? Who will you call? What will you do with the hardest moments? Having a basic plan for the immediate aftermath reduces the paralysis that can follow a major life change.

Post-separation boundaries. What contact will you have with your partner? What topics are and aren't appropriate? How will co-parenting communication be handled if applicable?

Take your time with this plan. You don't need to complete it in one sitting. And completing it doesn't mean you have to act on it immediately. The plan is a tool, one that gives you the clarity to move forward when you're ready, at whatever pace feels right.

Wrapping Up

Leaving a CPTSD-affected relationship can be done with care, integrity, and compassion. It requires preparation (financial, legal, logistical, and emotional), honest communication, and a willingness to sit with the guilt and grief that will inevitably follow. You are not abandoning a helpless person. You are making a decision about your own life after sustained effort and honest assessment. The guilt that follows is a reflection of your empathy, not evidence that you're wrong. The first months will be difficult, and the adjustment is non-linear, but research consistently shows that people who leave chronically distressing relationships report improved wellbeing over time. Rebuilding your life after is real work that deserves professional support and patience with yourself. The compassionate exit plan gives you a structured way to move forward with clarity and self-respect. Whatever the future holds, the decision to prioritize your own sustainability is not selfish. It is the foundation on which any good life is built.

Chapter 9 Getting Support Right Now

Whatever you decide about your relationship, one thing is not optional: you need support. Not eventually. Not when things settle down. Now.

If you've been the person who manages crises, absorbs emotional storms, researches treatment options, and holds the household together, you already know what it looks like to marshal resources for someone else. This chapter asks you to do the same thing for yourself. Because the truth is, you've likely spent so long being someone else's support system that the idea of building one for yourself may feel unfamiliar, even indulgent. It isn't. It is a basic requirement for getting through this with your health and clarity intact.

This chapter provides concrete, actionable resources. Some are for emergencies. Some are for the longer process of rebuilding. All of them are here because you deserve someone in your corner too.

If You Need Help Right Now

If you are in immediate physical danger, call 911 (in the United States) or your local emergency number. Do not wait. Do not try to de-escalate alone. Your safety comes first, regardless of what is causing the danger.

If you are experiencing domestic violence or coercive control, the National Domestic Violence Hotline is available 24 hours a day, seven days a week at 1-800-799-7233 (SAFE). You can also text START to 88788 or chat online at thehotline.org. Trained advocates can help you safety plan, connect you with local shelters, and assist with immediate needs. If you are outside the United States, the International Directory of Domestic Violence Agencies at hotpeachpages.net provides country-specific resources.

If you are experiencing thoughts of suicide or self-harm, the 988 Suicide and Crisis Lifeline is available by calling or texting 988 in the United States. The Crisis Text Line is available by texting HOME to 741741. For international resources, the International Association for Suicide Prevention maintains a directory at iasp.info/resources/Crisis_Centres.

If children are at risk of harm, contact your local child protective services agency or call the Childhelp National Child Abuse Hotline at 1-800-422-4453.

If you need immediate mental health support, many communities have mobile crisis teams that can come to you. Contact your local 211 service (dial 211 in the United States) for information about crisis resources in your area. Many insurance providers also offer 24-hour nurse or mental health lines listed on the back of your insurance card.

These resources are here because crises don't wait for convenient timing. If any of the situations above apply to you, please reach out before reading further. The rest of this book will still be here.

Finding Your Own Therapist

If you take one action after reading this book, let it be this: get your own therapist. Not a couples therapist (though that may be appropriate too, as we discussed in Chapter 7.0). Your own individual therapist, whose only job is to support you.

Why does this matter so much? Because you need a space where your experience is the centre of the conversation. In your daily life, your experience has likely been secondary to your partner's for a long time. In couples therapy, the focus is on the relationship. You need a room where the question is simply: how are you? What do you need? What do you want?

What to look for in a therapist:

Trauma-informed training. You've been living in close proximity to trauma, and you may have developed your own stress responses. A therapist who understands secondary traumatic stress, compassion fatigue, and the dynamics of trauma-affected relationships will be able to help you in ways that a general therapist may not. Look for clinicians with training in EMDR, somatic experiencing, or trauma-focused CBT, even if you are not the one with the primary trauma diagnosis.

Experience with partner dynamics. A therapist who has worked with partners of people with mental health conditions will understand the specific pressures you face: the guilt, the identity erosion, the caretaker role, the difficulty of setting boundaries with someone you love. This experience makes a meaningful difference in the quality of support you receive.

Neutrality about your relationship decision. A good therapist will not pressure you to stay or leave. They will help you think clearly, process your emotions, and arrive at your own conclusion. If a therapist makes you feel that you should stay because leaving would be "abandonment," or that you should leave immediately without adequate processing, consider whether that therapist is truly serving your needs.

Red flags in therapists: dismissing your experience ("your partner has the real problem, you're just stressed"), over-identifying with the CPTSD partner ("you need to understand that their behaviour isn't their fault" without acknowledging its impact on you), or pressuring you to make a particular decision about your relationship.

Affording therapy. Cost is a real barrier, and pretending otherwise helps no one. Options to explore: sliding scale fees (many therapists offer reduced rates based on income), community mental health centres (which provide services on a sliding scale or at no cost), online therapy platforms such as BetterHelp or Talkspace (which can be more affordable than in-person sessions), university training clinics (where graduate students provide therapy under supervision at reduced rates), and your employer's Employee Assistance Program (EAP), which typically offers a set number of free sessions. The Open Path Collective (openpathcollective.org) maintains a directory of therapists offering sessions between thirty and eighty dollars.

Your first sessions. Expect to spend the first one or two sessions giving your therapist the context of your situation. You may feel the urge to make sure they understand your partner's perspective too. Notice that urge. It's the caretaker pattern showing up in the therapy room. Your therapist needs to understand your experience. Your partner's perspective is your partner's therapist's job.

Reflection prompt: What has stopped you from getting your own therapist so far? Is that obstacle real, or is it the pattern of putting yourself last?

Finding Your People

Professional support is essential, but it is not the only kind of support you need. Peers who understand what you're going through provide something that therapists cannot: the experience of being deeply, specifically understood by someone who has lived it.

Support groups for partners of people with CPTSD, trauma histories, or mental health conditions can be found both online and in person. Organizations such as the National Alliance on Mental Illness (NAMI) offer support groups specifically for family members and partners. Online forums on platforms such as Reddit (communities like r/CPTSDpartners) and dedicated Facebook groups can provide connection and validation.

There is real power in hearing someone describe your exact experience without having to explain the background. The relief of saying "my partner did this and I felt this" and having someone respond with recognition rather than confusion is itself a form of healing. Research on peer support in caregiving contexts shows that participation in peer groups reduces feelings of isolation, improves coping, and decreases psychological distress (Chien et al., 2004).

But a caution is warranted. Online forums and support groups vary widely in quality and tone. Some are genuinely supportive spaces where partners help each other think clearly and maintain compassion for both themselves and their partners. Others can become echo chambers where venting replaces processing, where extreme positions are reinforced, and where nuance gets lost. If a group consistently leaves you feeling worse rather than better, more hopeless rather than more clear, or more angry without constructive direction, it may not be the right fit.

Building your personal support team is broader than finding a support group. Think about the different kinds of support you need and who in your life can provide each one.

The friend who listens. Someone who will let you talk without jumping to advice or judgment. The person you can call at nine in the evening when the house is quiet and the confusion hits.

The friend who tells you the truth. Someone who knows you well enough and loves you enough to say the uncomfortable thing. The person who will gently point out when you're making excuses or minimizing your own needs.

The friend who makes you laugh. Someone who reminds you that you are more than this situation. The person who takes you out of the crisis mindset and reconnects you with the part of yourself that isn't defined by your partner's condition.

You may not have all three right now. Part of this process is noticing which kinds of support are missing and beginning to fill those gaps.

Consider Oswin (name changed), who described building his support network after years of isolation. "I'd pushed everyone away. Not deliberately. But when your life revolves around managing someone else's crises, you stop calling friends. You cancel plans. You don't have the energy. When I finally started reaching out again, I was terrified. But the people who mattered came back. My college roommate, my sister, my old neighbour. They'd been waiting. They just didn't know how to get through."

Reflection prompt: If you made a list of three people you could call this week, who would be on it? What's stopping you from calling them?

Educating Yourself Wisely

Knowledge is a genuine resource. Understanding CPTSD, attachment dynamics, boundaries, and relationship patterns (the kind of understanding you've been building throughout this book) gives you language for your experience and a foundation for making decisions.

Recommended books that partners have found particularly useful include: *Complex PTSD: From Surviving to Thriving* by Pete Walker (2013), which provides the clearest accessible overview of CPTSD; *Codependent No More* by Melody Beattie (2022), which addresses the caregiving patterns that develop in relationships with people struggling with their mental health; *Set Boundaries, Find Peace* by Nedra Glennon Tawwab (2021), which offers practical guidance on establishing and maintaining boundaries; and *The Body Keeps the Score* by Bessel van der Kolk (2014), which explains how trauma affects the body and brain.

Podcasts and online resources can supplement reading. The "Therapy Chat" and "Psychology in Seattle" podcasts frequently address attachment, trauma, and relationship dynamics from professional perspectives. The website Out of the FOG (outofthefog.website) provides information specifically for people dealing with personality disorder and trauma dynamics in their relationships.

And here's a note that deserves emphasis: there is a point at which research becomes avoidance. If you've read twenty books, listened to a hundred podcasts, and joined multiple online communities but haven't taken any action in your own life (starting therapy, setting a boundary, having a conversation), the information gathering may have become a way to feel productive without actually changing anything. Research on procrastination through information-seeking suggests that excessive preparation can serve as an avoidance strategy, particularly when the action being avoided is emotionally difficult (Steel, 2007). At some point, you know enough. The next step is not more reading. It's doing.

Reflection prompt: Have you been using research as a way to prepare for action, or as a way to avoid it?

Someone in Your Corner

You have likely spent years being your partner's advocate, translator, and defender. You've explained their behaviour to confused family members. You've mediated between your partner and the world. You've absorbed criticism on their behalf and fought for their right to be understood.

Who has been doing that for you?

The isolation that CPTSD relationships create is one of their most damaging features. It happens gradually: you cancel plans because your partner is having a bad day, you stop sharing details with friends because the situation feels too complicated to explain, you pull away from family because their concern feels like criticism of your partner. Over time, your world contracts until it contains mainly you and your partner, and the very support structures that could help you assess your situation are no longer available.

Breaking that isolation is an act of reclaiming your own life. It starts with one conversation, one phone call, one honest answer to "how are you?" instead of the reflexive "I'm fine."

You don't have to explain your entire situation to receive support. You don't have to justify your feelings or your decisions. You just have to let someone in far enough to see that you need help. And then let them help.

As we discussed in Chapter 5.0, the erosion of self-trust is one of the most significant effects of living in a CPTSD-affected relationship. Asking for help is a direct counter to that erosion. It says: my experience matters, my needs are real, and I am allowed to receive care as well as give it.

Consider Kenrick (name changed), who described the moment he asked for help. "I called my brother. I hadn't really talked to him about any of this in years. I just said, 'I need to tell you what's been going on.' And I talked for an hour. He didn't fix anything. He didn't have solutions. But when I hung up, I felt ten pounds lighter. Someone knew. Someone saw me. That mattered more than I expected."

My Support Map

This chapter's reflection exercise asks you to map your current support system and identify what's missing.

Draw a simple diagram with yourself at the centre. Around you, place the people and resources currently in your life that provide some form of support. Include: professionals (therapist, doctor, attorney), close relationships (friends, family members), peer support (groups, online communities), and personal resources (activities, practices, places that restore you).

Now look at the map. Where are the gaps? Is there professional support missing? Peer connection? Trusted friends who know the full picture?

For each gap, write one concrete step you could take in the next two weeks to begin filling it. Not a complete solution. Just one step.

This map is a living document. As you move through whatever comes next, update it. Add resources as you find them. Let it remind you, on the hardest days, that you are building a structure of support around yourself, and that structure is how you get through this.

Essential Points

Support is not optional during this process. Crisis resources are available right now if you need them, and reaching out to them is a sign of clarity, not weakness. Individual therapy for yourself is the single most important step you can take, and options for affordable therapy are more available than many people realize. Peer support provides specific, lived understanding that professional support alone cannot offer, but online communities should be evaluated for quality and tone. Educating yourself about CPTSD and relationship dynamics is useful up to a point, but there is a line where research becomes avoidance, and recognizing that line matters. Breaking the isolation that CPTSD relationships create is an essential act of self-reclamation, and it begins with one honest conversation. You have been someone else's advocate for a long time. It is time to add yourself to that list.

Chapter 10 Deciding from Strength

You don't have to decide today. That sentence may be the most important one in this entire book.

The pressure to make the "right" decision, to figure this out, to land on an answer and commit to it, is real. It comes from inside you (the exhaustion of living in limbo), from outside you (friends and family asking "so what are you going to do?"), and from the situation itself (the sense that every day you don't decide is another day lost). But a decision made from exhaustion, guilt, or crisis is rarely a good one. What you want is to decide from the clearest, strongest, most self-connected version of yourself. Not the version that hasn't slept. Not the version that just survived another terrible argument. Not the version whose guilt is louder than their own voice.

This final chapter is about getting to that version of yourself, and then trusting what they tell you.

Making Decisions That Stick

Traditional decision-making tools don't work well for a choice like this. A list of advantages and disadvantages fails because the items aren't comparable: "I love this person" and "I'm losing my health" don't belong on the same scale. Logical analysis fails because relationships aren't logical, and the feelings involved don't reduce neatly to data points. Seeking consensus from friends and family fails because they can see only fragments of the full picture.

What works better is decision-making rooted in values and vision rather than calculation.

Values-based assessment. In Chapter 5.0, you identified your core values. Return to them now. What does your best life look like when it's organized around those values? Not your partner's best life. Not your children's best life (though their wellbeing is deeply relevant). Your best life. Can that life exist within this relationship? Not the fantasy version of the relationship, but the realistic version, given everything you now know about what can change (Chapter 4.0) and what the restructured approach would require (Chapter 7.0). If the answer is yes, staying may be the right choice. If the answer is no, that is important information.

The two futures visualization. Find a quiet moment. Close your eyes. Visualize yourself one year from now, having decided to stay and fully committed to the restructured approach outlined in Chapter 7.0. What does your daily life look like? How do you feel when you wake up? What is your relationship with your partner like? What is your relationship with yourself like? Sit with that picture for several minutes.

Now visualize yourself one year from now, having left. You've gone through the difficult months described in Chapter 8.0. What does your daily life look like now? How do you feel? What has been lost? What has been gained?

Neither picture will be entirely comfortable. Both will contain pain. The question is: which picture feels more like the life you want to live?

The rocking chair test. Imagine yourself at eighty, looking back on this period of your life. Which decision are you more at peace with? Which one would the eighty-year-old version of you understand and respect? This exercise doesn't produce certainty, but it often cuts through the noise of present-moment anxiety and connects you with a deeper sense of what matters.

Distinguishing intuition from anxiety. Both intuition and anxiety produce strong gut feelings. The difference is in their quality. Anxiety is noisy, urgent, and often contradictory (it screams "leave!" one day and "stay!" the next). Intuition is quieter, more consistent, and often accompanied by a sense of settled knowing rather than frantic certainty. Research on the role of intuition in decision-making suggests that gut feelings are most reliable when they are informed by significant experience with the domain in question (Dane and Pratt, 2007). You have significant experience with this relationship. Your intuition has data. The challenge is hearing it underneath the anxiety.

Reflection prompt: When the noise quiets down, in the moments between crises, what does your gut consistently say?

Finding the Clear Moments

There is something that partners in CPTSD relationships often describe: the **clarity window**. It's a moment, sometimes brief, sometimes lasting hours or days, when the confusion lifts and you see your situation with sudden, honest clearness. You know, in that moment, what you need to do. The picture is sharp. The noise is gone.

And then the window closes. Guilt floods in, or fear, or a good day with your partner, or a crisis that demands all your attention. And the clarity dissolves back into confusion.

Learning to recognize and trust these moments is one of the most important skills you can develop during this process.

Clarity often arrives after a crisis, because crises strip away the rationalizations and coping mechanisms that normally buffer you from the raw truth of your situation. The problem is that post-crisis clarity is also tangled with adrenaline and emotional reactivity, which can make it difficult to trust. The key distinction: clarity feels calm and settled, even when what it reveals is painful. Reactivity feels urgent and charged. If you find yourself thinking "I need to get out of here right now, tonight," that may be reactivity. If you find yourself thinking "I know, quietly and clearly, that this relationship cannot continue as it is," that is more likely clarity.

How to access clarity without waiting for a crisis:

Journaling for clarity. Specific prompts designed to cut through confusion: "What am I most afraid of in this situation?" "If I knew that both choices would eventually be okay, which would I choose?" "What would I tell my daughter or son to do in my situation?" "What am I pretending not to know?" Write without editing. Write without trying to be fair to your partner. Let the words come without filtering them through the lens of their needs.

Physical distance. When you can, spend time away from your partner and your shared home. A weekend at a friend's house. A few days with family. Even an afternoon in a park, alone with your own thoughts. Research on the effect of physical environment on decision-making confirms that spatial distance from a problem can facilitate broader, more abstract thinking, which supports better long-term decision-making (Trope and Liberman, 2010). Many partners report that their clearest thinking happens when they are physically away from the environment where the CPTSD dynamics play out.

Somatic awareness. As we discussed in Chapter 5.0, your body carries information that your mind may be arguing with. When you consider staying, what happens in your body? When you consider leaving? Tension, nausea, a sense of heaviness, a feeling of lightness, tears that arrive without explanation: these are all forms of data.

Consider Bramwell (name changed), who discovered his clarity during a work trip. "I was away for five days. By day three, I realized I was sleeping through the night. By day four, I noticed I was laughing at things that weren't even that funny. My whole body felt different. And on the flight home, I felt it all start to tighten again. That contrast told me more than two years of therapy had. My body knew what my mind was still debating."

Reflection prompt: When was the last time you experienced a moment of clarity about your situation? What did it tell you? What happened to that clarity afterward?

Taking Your Time

You are allowed to take time with this decision. You are also allowed to set a framework around that time so it doesn't stretch into indefinite avoidance.

Setting a private timeline means giving yourself a specific period during which you will actively work on gathering information, building support, trying the approaches described in this book, and paying close attention to what you learn. It might be three months. It might be six. It might be a year. The timeline is yours. It doesn't need to be shared with your partner. Its purpose is to provide you with structure: a defined period of intentional observation and effort, after which you will reassess honestly.

The difference between taking time and avoiding the decision is this: taking time involves active engagement (therapy, conversations, boundary-setting, honest self-assessment). Avoiding the decision involves passive drifting (doing nothing different, hoping things will change on their own, refusing to engage with the questions this book has raised). If your "taking time" involves concrete actions and genuine reflection, it is valid and valuable. If it involves none of those things, you may be using time as a buffer against a conclusion you've already reached.

Permission to change your mind. This applies in both
directions. If you decide to stay and later realize it's not working,
you are allowed to change course. If you decide to leave and
later discover that genuine change has occurred, you are allowed
to reconsider. Decisions about relationships are not blood oaths.
They are assessments made with the best information available
at the time, and they can be revisited as new information
emerges.

Permission to make an imperfect decision. There is no perfect
answer to the question this book addresses. Both staying and
leaving carry costs. Both involve loss. Both require courage. The
goal is not to find the painless option (it doesn't exist) but to find
the option that aligns most closely with your values, your needs,
and the life you want to live. That decision will be imperfect.
Make it anyway.

*Reflection prompt: If you gave yourself a private timeline of six
months to gather information and make a decision, what would
you want to know by the end of that period?*

When the Answer Won't Come

Some readers will reach this point in the book and still not know
what to do. If that's you, here's what to understand: not knowing
is not failure.

Living in the "I don't know" with integrity means continuing to
show up for your own life, maintaining your boundaries,
engaging with your support system, and staying honest with
yourself, even without a clear direction. It means treating the
uncertainty as a season rather than a permanent state, one that
will eventually yield to clarity if you keep doing the work.

Temporary structures can help when the bigger decision
remains unresolved. A trial separation (with clear terms and a
defined timeframe) gives both partners the experience of

physical distance and can provide information that is impossible to access from inside the shared dynamic. New agreements within the relationship (as described in Chapter 7.0) create a defined experiment: if these changes are made, how does the relationship function? Time-limited commitments ("I will give this restructured approach six months") allow you to invest genuinely without committing indefinitely.

The information you still need. If you don't know what to decide, ask yourself: what information would change that? Is it information about your partner's willingness to engage with treatment? About your own ability to maintain boundaries? About what life on your own would actually feel like? Name the missing information, and then figure out how to get it. The answer to "what do I need to know?" often reveals the next step, even when the final decision remains unclear.

When indecision is the decision. Sometimes, not deciding is itself a choice. If you have been "deciding" for years without reaching a conclusion, the indecision may be functioning as a form of staying. That isn't necessarily wrong, but it's worth naming honestly. If your indecision is keeping you in a situation that is causing ongoing harm, then the indecision is not neutral. It is the mechanism by which the status quo continues.

Reflection prompt: What information would you need in order to feel ready to make a decision? How could you get that information?

Whatever You Choose

If you decide to stay: you are choosing courage. Staying in a CPTSD-affected relationship with new structure, honest agreements, professional support, and clear boundaries is hard work. It requires you to show up differently, to hold your partner accountable compassionately, and to protect your own wellbeing while investing in the relationship. The chapters behind you have given you a framework for doing this sustainably. Use that framework. Revisit it. Return to the exercises when you need them. And remember that staying is a renewable choice, one you make again each day, and one you can unmake if the conditions you set are not met.

If you decide to leave: you are choosing honesty. Leaving someone you love because the relationship is unsustainable is one of the hardest things a person can do. It will hurt. It will cost you things you value. It will require you to sit with guilt and grief and the judgment of people who don't understand. But it will also open a door to a life where your needs, your health, and your future are no longer secondary considerations. The preparation and guidance in Chapter 8.0 will help you leave with care and integrity. You are not abandoning anyone. You are reclaiming yourself.

If you're still deciding: you are choosing patience with yourself. There is no deadline for this decision, and rushing it to escape the discomfort of uncertainty would not serve you. Keep doing the work: therapy, support, honest self-assessment, boundary-setting. Keep listening to the clarity when it arrives and noticing the fear when it interferes. The answer will come. It may come quietly, without fanfare, on an ordinary Tuesday when you suddenly know what you've known for a while. Trust that process.

And underneath all three paths, there is a truth that applies to every reader of this book: you are already stronger than you think. You have been doing one of the hardest things a person can do: loving someone through their deepest pain while trying not to lose yourself in the process. The fact that you're here, reading these words, thinking about your future, asking honest questions about your life, is evidence of a strength that deserves your own recognition.

Your life matters. Not as an appendix to someone else's story. Not as a support structure for someone else's healing. Your life, in its own right, with its own needs and its own trajectory, matters. Whatever you decide, carry that with you.

The Letter to Your Future Self

Write a letter to the version of yourself who exists one year from now. Write it from wherever you stand today: the uncertainty, the exhaustion, the hope, the fear, all of it.

Tell that future self what you're feeling right now. Tell them what you're most afraid of. Tell them what you're hoping for. Tell them what you've learned from this book, from your own reflection, and from the honest inventory of your relationship.

Ask them: did I make the right call? Are you okay? Are you glad I found the courage to face this honestly?

And then seal it. Put a date on it twelve months from now. When that date arrives, open it and read what you wrote. The distance between who you are today and who you'll be then is the space in which your decision will live and your life will continue to unfold.

You don't need to have the answer right now. You just need to keep being honest. The rest will follow.

Appendix A Safety Assessment Checklist

This checklist is designed to help you assess your physical, emotional, and psychological safety within your relationship. It is not a diagnostic tool. It is a structured way to look at your situation honestly and determine whether safety planning is needed.

Answer each question based on your actual experience, not on what you think the "right" answer should be.

Physical Safety

Has your partner ever hit, shoved, grabbed, slapped, or thrown objects at you?

Has your partner ever physically blocked you from leaving a room or a space?

Has your partner ever damaged property (punching walls, breaking objects) during conflict?

Has your partner ever driven recklessly or used a vehicle to intimidate you?

Has your partner ever hurt or threatened to hurt a pet?

Are there weapons in the home, and has your partner ever referenced them during an argument or conflict?

Coercive Control

Does your partner monitor your phone, email, or social media accounts?

Does your partner control the household finances in ways that limit your access to money?

Does your partner restrict who you can see, where you can go, or what you can do?

Does your partner require you to check in or report your whereabouts regularly?

Does your partner make decisions about your body, appearance, or health without your input?

Has your partner isolated you from friends, family, or other support networks?

Emotional and Psychological Safety

Does your partner regularly tell you that your perceptions are wrong or that events didn't happen the way you remember?

Does your partner threaten to harm themselves if you set boundaries, express concerns, or discuss leaving?

Does your partner use personal information you shared in vulnerability against you during arguments?

Does your partner humiliate, belittle, or mock you, either privately or in front of others?

Does your partner blame you for their emotional reactions, episodes, or behaviour?

Do you feel afraid of your partner's reaction when you express a need or disagreement?

Safety of Children

Has your partner physically harmed a child in the household?

Are children frequently exposed to your partner's emotional dysregulation, verbal aggression, or threatening behaviour?

Has your partner used children as leverage (threatening custody, turning children against you)?

Do children in the household show signs of fear, anxiety, or behavioural changes related to the home environment?

Your Internal Experience

Do you feel safe in your own home most of the time?

Can you be yourself without monitoring your words or behaviour?

Do you have the freedom to make your own choices about your daily life?

Can you express disagreement or raise concerns without fearing retaliation?

Interpreting Your Answers

If you answered yes to any question in the Physical Safety section, your safety may be at immediate risk. Please contact the National Domestic Violence Hotline at 1-800-799-7233 or text START to 88788.

If you answered yes to multiple questions in the Coercive Control section, your relationship may involve patterns of abuse that require professional assessment and safety planning. A domestic violence advocate can help you evaluate your situation and develop a plan.

If you answered yes to questions in the Emotional and Psychological Safety section, your relationship involves dynamics that are causing harm. Individual therapy and, depending on the severity, professional safety planning are recommended.

If you answered yes to any question in the Safety of Children section, the wellbeing of children in your household is at risk. Contact the Childhelp National Child Abuse Hotline at 1-800-422-4453 for guidance.

If your answers in the Your Internal Experience section are consistently no, your situation warrants serious attention regardless of how the other sections scored.

Creating a Safety Plan

If your assessment indicates that safety planning is needed, the following steps are recommended.

Identify a safe place you can go quickly if needed (a friend's home, a family member's home, a shelter).

Keep important documents in a secure location outside the home or in a bag that is ready to go: identification, financial documents, custody or legal documents, medical records, and a list of emergency contacts.

Inform at least one trusted person about your situation and your plan.

Save the National Domestic Violence Hotline number in your phone under a neutral contact name.

If there are children involved, include them in your safety plan (where they will go, who will care for them, what they need to bring).

Contact a domestic violence advocate for professional help developing a comprehensive safety plan tailored to your specific situation.

A safety plan is not a commitment to leave. It is a commitment to being prepared. Having a plan does not mean you have decided to go. It means you have decided that your safety matters enough to plan for.

Appendix B The Partner's Bill of Rights

Regardless of your partner's diagnosis, history, or condition, you are entitled to the following in any relationship. These are not aspirations. They are baseline requirements for a partnership in which both people can function with dignity.

You have the right to physical safety. No diagnosis, trauma history, or emotional state justifies physical violence against you. You are entitled to live without fear of being hit, shoved, grabbed, or physically intimidated.

You have the right to emotional safety. You are entitled to express your feelings, raise concerns, and share your experience without being punished, mocked, or silenced. Your emotional reality is valid even when it is inconvenient for someone else.

You have the right to your own perceptions. You are entitled to trust what you see, hear, remember, and feel. No one has the right to systematically tell you that your perceptions are wrong as a way of maintaining control or avoiding accountability.

You have the right to have needs. Your needs for connection, stability, affection, companionship, and support are legitimate. They do not become less legitimate because your partner also has needs. Two sets of needs can coexist, and yours do not automatically rank below theirs.

You have the right to set boundaries. You are entitled to say no, to limit what you will accept, and to enforce consequences when boundaries are violated. Boundaries are not cruelty. They are the structures that make any healthy relationship possible.

You have the right to your own identity. You are more than a caretaker, a stabilizing force, or a support system. You are a whole person with your own interests, friendships, goals, and inner life. You are entitled to maintain that identity within the relationship.

You have the right to honesty. You are entitled to truthful communication from your partner. Deception, manipulation, and the deliberate withholding of information are not acceptable, regardless of the emotional state that prompts them.

You have the right to make your own choices. You are entitled to decide what you do, where you go, who you see, and how you spend your time. No one has the right to control these decisions, whether through explicit demands or through emotional consequences that function as control.

You have the right to be imperfect. You are allowed to have bad days, lose patience, say the wrong thing, and fall short of the impossible standard of constant compassion. You are a human being, not a therapeutic intervention.

You have the right to happiness. Your happiness is not a selfish pursuit. It is a legitimate need that deserves to be weighted alongside every other consideration in your relationship. You are not required to be perpetually unhappy so that someone else can be marginally more comfortable.

You have the right to leave. You are entitled to end a relationship that is not working for you. This right is not contingent on your partner's diagnosis, their emotional state, or anyone else's opinion about your decision. You are allowed to choose your own future.

You have the right to stay. You are equally entitled to choose to remain in the relationship, with new structures and agreements, if that choice is made from clarity rather than guilt.

No one has the right to pressure you into leaving, just as no one has the right to pressure you into staying.

You have the right to take your time. You are allowed to not know what to do. You are allowed to sit with uncertainty. You are allowed to change your mind. The decision you're facing is one of the most complex a person can encounter, and you are entitled to give it the time it deserves.

You have the right to support. You are entitled to professional help, peer support, and the care of people who see you and your situation clearly. Asking for help is not weakness. It is the action of someone who takes their own life seriously.

This list is not negotiable. It is not conditional on anyone else's behaviour, diagnosis, or circumstances. These rights are yours simply because you are a person in a relationship, and they deserve to be honoured.

Appendix C Recommended Resources

Books

Walker, P. (2013). *Complex PTSD: From Surviving to Thriving.* Azure Coyote Publishing. The most accessible and widely recommended guide to understanding CPTSD from the inside. Essential reading for both the partner with CPTSD and the partner supporting them.

Herman, J. L. (1992). *Trauma and Recovery: The Aftermath of Violence, from Domestic Abuse to Political Terror.* Basic Books. The foundational text in the field of complex trauma. Academic but readable, and essential for understanding the three-stage model of recovery referenced throughout this book.

Van der Kolk, B. A. (2014). *The Body Keeps the Score: Brain, Mind, and Body in the Healing of Trauma.* Viking. A comprehensive overview of how trauma affects the body and brain, and the range of treatments available. Particularly useful for understanding the neurobiological components of your partner's experience.

Beattie, M. (2022). *Codependent No More: How to Stop Controlling Others and Start Caring for Yourself* (revised ed.). Hazelden Publishing. A classic text on the caregiving patterns that develop in relationships where one partner is struggling. Directly relevant to the identity and boundary questions addressed in Chapters 5 and 6.

Tawwab, N. G. (2021). *Set Boundaries, Find Peace: A Guide to Reclaiming Yourself.* TarcherPerigee. Practical, accessible guidance on establishing and maintaining boundaries. Useful as

a companion to the boundary work described in Chapters 7 and
8.

Bancroft, L. (2002). *Why Does He Do That? Inside the Minds of
Angry and Controlling Men*. Berkley Books. Essential reading
for anyone assessing whether their relationship involves abuse.
While focused on male abusers, the dynamics described apply
across genders. Directly relevant to Chapter 3.

Johnson, S. M. (2008). *Hold Me Tight: Seven Conversations for
a Lifetime of Love*. Little, Brown. An introduction to
Emotionally Focused Therapy for couples. Useful for partners
who decide to stay and want to understand the attachment-based
approach to couples work.

Levine, P. A. (2010). *In an Unspoken Voice: How the Body
Releases Trauma and Restores Goodness*. North Atlantic Books.
An accessible introduction to Somatic Experiencing and the role
of the body in trauma recovery.

Schwartz, R. C. (2021). *No Bad Parts: Healing Trauma and
Restoring Wholeness with the Internal Family Systems Model*.
Sounds True. An introduction to IFS, one of the therapeutic
modalities discussed in Chapter 4. Useful for understanding how
parts-based therapy works and what it can offer.

Podcasts

"Therapy Chat" hosted by Laura Reagan, LCSW-C. Covers
trauma, attachment, and therapeutic approaches in an accessible
format. Frequent episodes on CPTSD, relationship dynamics,
and boundaries.

"Psychology in Seattle" hosted by Dr. Kirk Honda. Thoughtful
explorations of relationship dynamics, attachment theory, and
therapeutic concepts. Balanced and professional perspective.

"The Place We Find Ourselves" hosted by Adam Young, LCSW. Focused specifically on attachment and trauma, with episodes that help listeners understand how childhood experiences shape adult relationships.

"Unfck Your Brain" hosted by Kara Loewentheil. Focused on cognitive patterns, self-concept, and decision-making. Useful for partners working on reclaiming their own perspective and identity.

Websites and Online Resources

Out of the FOG (outofthefog.website). Information and support for people dealing with personality disorder and trauma dynamics in their relationships. Includes a toolbox section with practical coping strategies.

The National Domestic Violence Hotline (thehotline.org). 24/7 support via phone (1-800-799-7233), text (START to 88788), and online chat. Also provides educational resources about relationship dynamics, safety planning, and coercive control.

NAMI (nami.org). The National Alliance on Mental Illness offers support groups for family members and partners, educational programs, and a helpline (1-800-950-6264).

Psychology Today Therapist Directory (psychologytoday.com/us/therapists). Searchable directory of therapists with filters for specialization (trauma, PTSD, relationship issues), insurance, and location.

Open Path Collective (openpathcollective.org). A directory of therapists offering sessions at reduced rates (thirty to eighty dollars per session). Useful for partners seeking affordable individual therapy.

BetterHelp (betterhelp.com) and Talkspace (talkspace.com). Online therapy platforms that can provide more affordable and accessible options, particularly in areas with limited local therapists.

Crisis Hotlines and Support Services

National Domestic Violence Hotline: 1-800-799-7233 or text START to 88788 (United States)

988 Suicide and Crisis Lifeline: Call or text 988 (United States)

Crisis Text Line: Text HOME to 741741 (United States)

Childhelp National Child Abuse Hotline: 1-800-422-4453 (United States)

SAMHSA National Helpline: 1-800-662-4357 (United States, substance abuse and mental health referrals)

International Association for Suicide Prevention: iasp.info/resources/Crisis_Centres (international directory)

Hot Peach Pages: hotpeachpages.net (international directory of domestic violence agencies)

Online Communities

r/CPTSDpartners (Reddit). A community specifically for partners of people with CPTSD. Moderated and generally supportive, though quality varies by thread.

CPTSD-specific Facebook groups. Search for groups specifically for partners (not general CPTSD groups, which may not centre the partner's experience). Evaluate for tone and moderation quality before engaging deeply.

NAMI Connection Recovery Support Groups. Free, peer-led support groups for anyone affected by mental health conditions. Available in person and online. Details at nami.org/support-education.

A note on online communities: as discussed in Chapter 9, the value of these spaces varies widely. Use them for connection and validation, but assess regularly whether they are helping you think more clearly or reinforcing patterns that keep you stuck.

Appendix D A Note for the CPTSD Partner

If you're reading this, it's likely because your partner has been reading this book. Or perhaps you found it yourself. Either way, this note is for you, and it's written with the same compassion that runs through every chapter.

What This Book Is

This book was written for partners of people with CPTSD who are trying to figure out whether to stay or leave. It takes their experience seriously. It validates their pain. It gives them permission to have needs, set boundaries, and make decisions about their own lives.

Reading that sentence may be painful. It may feel like a threat. It may feel like the beginning of the very abandonment you've feared your whole life. That reaction makes sense given what you've been through. But please stay with this for a moment, because what follows is important.

What This Book Is Not

This book is not an attack on you. It does not portray people with CPTSD as monsters, as hopeless cases, or as people who don't deserve love. Throughout these pages, your trauma is acknowledged as real, its origins are treated with compassion, and your capacity for growth and healing is affirmed.

This book does not tell your partner to leave. It helps them think clearly about a difficult situation so they can make the best decision for themselves. For some readers, that decision will be to stay and work on the relationship with renewed commitment.

For others, it will be to go. The book supports both paths equally.

This book does not say that your behaviour is your fault. It does say that your behaviour is your responsibility. There is a difference. You did not choose what happened to you. You did not choose to develop CPTSD. You did not choose the nervous system responses, the attachment patterns, or the emotional storms that your trauma created. None of that was your fault. But what you do with those responses now, whether you seek treatment, whether you take accountability for impact, whether you're willing to engage in the hard work of recovery, that is within your agency. And your partner has the right to factor your choices in those areas into their own decisions about the relationship.

What Your Partner Has Been Carrying

The person who brought this book home has been carrying something heavy. They've been living inside the secondary effects of your trauma: the unpredictability, the emotional intensity, the cycles of crisis and calm, the difficulty of never quite knowing which version of the day they'll walk into. They've likely done this with enormous love and patience, often at significant cost to their own health, identity, and wellbeing.

This is not said to make you feel guilty. It is said because your partner's experience deserves the same kind of honest acknowledgment that yours does. Two things are true at the same time: what happened to you was terrible and unfair, and the relational dynamics that your trauma creates are causing your partner genuine suffering. Both of those realities exist simultaneously, and neither cancels the other out.

Your partner's decision to read this book is not a betrayal. It is an act of courage. They are trying to figure out how to take care of themselves while continuing to care about you. The fact that they need a book to help them do that tells you something about how hard it's been.

An Invitation

If your partner decides to stay and work on the relationship with new structures and agreements (as described in Chapter 7.0 of this book), that's an opportunity. It means they haven't given up. But it also means things need to change. The dynamic that brought them to this book cannot continue as it was.

Engaging with that change might mean:

Committing to consistent, ongoing trauma therapy with a qualified professional. Not starting and stopping. Not going only after crises. Regular, sustained engagement with treatment.

Taking accountability for the impact of your behaviour, even when the behaviour was driven by trauma. Impact and intent are separate things. Your partner can understand that you didn't mean to cause harm and still need you to acknowledge that harm occurred.

Participating in couples therapy with a trauma-informed therapist, if both of you agree that it would be helpful and if your therapist assesses that it is safe and appropriate.

Working on the crisis plans, communication structures, and agreements your partner may propose. These aren't punishments. They're the scaffolding that makes the relationship sustainable for both of you.

Being willing to hear your partner's pain without making it about your own. This is perhaps the hardest thing this book asks of you, because your pain is real and it is loud and it has been with you for a long time. But your partner's pain is also real, and they need you to hold space for it alongside your own.

If Your Partner Decides to Leave

If your partner reaches the conclusion that they need to go, that will be devastating. It may feel like confirmation of every fear your trauma has ever generated: that you're too much, that nobody can stay, that you're fundamentally unlovable. Those beliefs are your trauma talking. They are not the truth.

Your partner's decision to leave is not about your worth. It is about their capacity. They have reached a limit. That limit is not a judgment of who you are. It is an honest assessment of what they can sustain.

You will survive this. You have survived worse. And the work of recovery, which was always yours to do regardless of whether this relationship continued, is still available to you.

Resources for Your Recovery

Your healing matters too. Here are resources specifically for CPTSD recovery:

Complex PTSD: From Surviving to Thriving by Pete Walker is the most widely recommended starting point for understanding CPTSD from the inside and developing practical tools for managing it.

The ISTSS (International Society for Traumatic Stress Studies) maintains a directory of clinicians who specialize in complex trauma treatment at istss.org.

EMDR, CPT, IFS, somatic experiencing, and schema therapy are all evidence-based approaches that have shown effectiveness for CPTSD. Ask potential therapists about their training in these specific modalities.

The 988 Suicide and Crisis Lifeline (call or text 988) is available if you are in crisis at any point during this process.

NAMI (nami.org) offers peer support groups and educational resources for people living with mental health conditions.

A Final Word

This book exists because your partner is in pain and because they love you enough to try to think clearly about what to do with that pain. The compassion you want them to extend to you is the same compassion this appendix is asking you to extend to them. Their pain counts too. Their needs are real too. And their right to a life that is sustainable and whole is just as legitimate as yours.

Whatever happens next, the invitation is the same for both of you: choose honesty, choose growth, and choose to treat your own healing as something that matters. Not because anyone else requires it, but because you deserve it.

References

Amato, P. R. (2010). Research on divorce: Continuing trends and new developments. *Journal of Marriage and Family, 72*(3), 650–666. doi:10.1111/j.1741-3737.2010.00723.x

Arkes, H. R., & Blumer, C. (1985). The psychology of sunk cost. *Organizational Behavior and Human Decision Processes, 35*(1), 124–140. doi:10.1016/0749-5978(85)90049-4

Arnsten, A. F. T. (2009). Stress signalling pathways that impair prefrontal cortex structure and function. *Nature Reviews Neuroscience, 10*(6), 410–422. doi:10.1038/nrn2648

Awad, A. G., & Voruganti, L. N. P. (2008). The burden of schizophrenia on caregivers: A review. *PharmacoEconomics, 26*(2), 149–162. doi:10.2165/00019053-200826020-00005

Bancroft, L. (2002). *Why does he do that? Inside the minds of angry and controlling men.* Berkley Books.

Bateman, A. W., & Fonagy, P. (2016). *Mentalization-based treatment for personality disorders: A practical guide.* Oxford University Press. doi:10.1093/med:psych/9780199680375.001.0001

Beattie, M. (2022). *Codependent no more: How to stop controlling others and start caring for yourself* (Revised and updated ed.). Spiegel & Grau.

Benazon, N. R., & Coyne, J. C. (2000). Living with a depressed spouse. *Journal of Family Psychology, 14*(1), 71–79. doi:10.1037/0893-3200.14.1.71

Bowlby, J. (1969). *Attachment and loss: Vol. 1. Attachment.* Basic Books.

Brassard, A., Dupuy, E., Bergeron, S., & Shaver, P. R. (2015). Attachment insecurities and women's sexual function and satisfaction: The mediating roles of sexual self-esteem, sexual anxiety, and sexual assertiveness. *Journal of Sex Research, 52*(1), 110–119. doi:10.1080/00224499.2013.838744

Bride, B. E. (2007). Prevalence of secondary traumatic stress among social workers. *Social Work, 52*(1), 63–70. doi:10.1093/sw/52.1.63

Chien, W. T., Norman, I., & Thompson, D. R. (2004). A randomized controlled trial of a mutual support group for family caregivers of patients with schizophrenia. *International Journal of Nursing Studies, 41*(6), 637–649. doi:10.1016/j.ijnurstu.2004.01.010

Cloitre, M., Courtois, C. A., Charuvastra, A., Carapezza, R., Stolbach, B. C., & Green, B. L. (2011). Treatment of complex PTSD: Results of the ISTSS expert clinician survey on best practices. *Journal of Traumatic Stress, 24*(6), 615–627. doi:10.1002/jts.20697

Cohen, S., & Wills, T. A. (1985). Stress, social support, and the buffering hypothesis. *Psychological Bulletin, 98*(2), 310–357. doi:10.1037/0033-2909.98.2.310

Critchley, H. D., & Garfinkel, S. N. (2017). Interoception and emotion. *Current Opinion in Psychology, 17*, 7–14. doi:10.1016/j.copsyc.2017.04.020

Cummings, E. M., & Davies, P. T. (2010). *Marital conflict and children: An emotional security perspective.* Guilford Press.

Dailey, R. M., Pfiester, A., Jin, B., Beck, G., & Clark, G. (2009). On-again/off-again dating relationships: How are they different from other dating relationships? *Personal Relationships, 16*(1), 23–47. doi:10.1111/j.1475-6811.2009.01208.x

Dane, E., & Pratt, M. G. (2007). Exploring intuition and its role in managerial decision making. *Academy of Management Review, 32*(1), 33–54. doi:10.5465/amr.2007.23463682

Davidson, R. J., & McEwen, B. S. (2012). Social influences on neuroplasticity: Stress and interventions to promote well-being. *Nature Neuroscience, 15*(5), 689–695. doi:10.1038/nn.3093

Dear, G. E., Roberts, C. M., & Lange, L. (2005). Defining codependency: A thematic analysis of published definitions. In S. Shohov (Ed.), *Advances in psychology research* (Vol. 34, pp. 189–205). Nova Science Publishers.

Dekel, R., & Monson, C. M. (2010). Military-related post-traumatic stress disorder and family relations: Current knowledge and future directions. *Aggression and Violent Behavior, 15*(4), 303–309. doi:10.1016/j.avb.2010.03.001

Dutton, D. G. (2007). *Rethinking domestic violence.* University of British Columbia Press.

Erickson, R. J. (2005). Why emotion work matters: Sex, gender, and the division of household labor. *Journal of Marriage and Family, 67*(2), 337–351. doi:10.1111/j.0022-2445.2005.00120.x

Figley, C. R. (2002). Compassion fatigue: Psychotherapists' chronic lack of self-care. *Journal of Clinical Psychology, 58*(11), 1433–1441. doi:10.1002/jclp.10090

Gottman, J. M., & Silver, N. (2015). *The seven principles for making marriage work* (2nd ed.). Harmony Books.

Henry, S. B., Smith, D. B., Archuleta, K. L., Sanders-Hahs, E., Goff, B. S. N., Reisbig, A. M. J., Schwerdtfeger, K. L., Bole, A., Hayes, E., Hoheisel, C. B., Bolen, J., & Scheer, T. (2011). Trauma and couples: Mechanisms in dyadic functioning.

Journal of Marital and Family Therapy, 37(3), 319–332. doi:10.1111/j.1752-0606.2010.00203.x

Herman, J. L. (1992). *Trauma and recovery: The aftermath of violence, from domestic abuse to political terror.* Basic Books.

Johnson, M. P. (2008). *A typology of domestic violence: Intimate terrorism, violent resistance, and situational couple violence.* Northeastern University Press.

Johnson, S. M. (2019). *Attachment theory in practice: Emotionally focused therapy (EFT) with individuals, couples, and families.* Guilford Press.

Kiecolt-Glaser, J. K., Preacher, K. J., MacCallum, R. C., Atkinson, C., Malarkey, W. B., & Glaser, R. (2003). Chronic stress and age-related increases in the proinflammatory cytokine IL-6. *Proceedings of the National Academy of Sciences, 100*(15), 9090–9095. doi:10.1073/pnas.1531903100

Levine, P. A. (2010). *In an unspoken voice: How the body releases trauma and restores goodness.* North Atlantic Books.

Lieberman, A. F., & Van Horn, P. (2008). *Psychotherapy with infants and young children: Repairing the effects of stress and trauma on early attachment.* Guilford Press.

Losada, A., Márquez-González, M., Knight, B. G., Yanguas, J., Sayegh, P., & Romero-Moreno, R. (2010). Psychosocial factors and caregivers' distress: Effects of familism and dysfunctional thoughts. *Aging & Mental Health, 14*(2), 193–202. doi:10.1080/13607860903167838

Main, M., & Hesse, E. (1990). Parents' unresolved traumatic experiences are related to infant disorganized attachment status: Is frightened and/or frightening parental behavior the linking mechanism? In M. T. Greenberg, D. Cicchetti, & E. M.

Cummings (Eds.), *Attachment in the preschool years: Theory, research, and intervention* (pp. 161–182). University of Chicago Press.

Maslach, C., & Leiter, M. P. (2016). Understanding the burnout experience: Recent research and its implications for psychiatry. *World Psychiatry, 15*(2), 103–111. doi:10.1002/wps.20311

Pennebaker, J. W., & Smyth, J. M. (2016). *Opening up by writing it down: How expressive writing improves health and eases emotional pain* (3rd ed.). Guilford Press.

Porges, S. W. (2011). *The polyvagal theory: Neurophysiological foundations of emotions, attachment, communication, and self-regulation.* W. W. Norton.

Prochaska, J. O., & DiClemente, C. C. (1983). Stages and processes of self-change of smoking: Toward an integrative model of change. *Journal of Consulting and Clinical Psychology, 51*(3), 390–395. doi:10.1037/0022-006X.51.3.390

Prescott, J., & Mackie, L. (2017). "You sort of go down a rabbit hole… you're just going to keep on searching": A qualitative study of searching online for pregnancy-related information during pregnancy. *Journal of Medical Internet Research, 19*(6), e194. doi:10.2196/jmir.6302

Resick, P. A., Monson, C. M., & Chard, K. M. (2017). *Cognitive processing therapy for PTSD: A comprehensive manual.* Guilford Press.

Revenson, T. A., Kayser, K., & Bodenmann, G. (Eds.). (2005). *Couples coping with stress: Emerging perspectives on dyadic coping.* American Psychological Association. doi:10.1037/11031-000

Sbarra, D. A., & Emery, R. E. (2005). The emotional sequelae of nonmarital relationship dissolution: Analysis of change and intraindividual variability over time. *Personal Relationships, 12*(2), 213–232. doi:10.1111/j.1350-4126.2005.00112.x

Schulz, R., Mendelsohn, A. B., Haley, W. E., Mahoney, D., Allen, R. S., Zhang, S., Thompson, L., & Belle, S. H. (2004). End-of-life care and the effects of bereavement on family caregivers of persons with dementia. *New England Journal of Medicine, 349*(20), 1936–1942. doi:10.1056/NEJMsa035373

Schwartz, R. C. (2021). *No bad parts: Healing trauma and restoring wholeness with the internal family systems model.* Sounds True.

Shapiro, F. (2018). *Eye movement desensitization and reprocessing (EMDR) therapy: Basic principles, protocols, and procedures* (3rd ed.). Guilford Press.

Siegel, D. J. (2012). *The developing mind: How relationships and the brain interact to shape who we are* (2nd ed.). Guilford Press.

Stark, E. (2007). *Coercive control: How men entrap women in personal life.* Oxford University Press. doi:10.1093/acprof:oso/9780195384048.001.0001

Steel, P. (2007). The nature of procrastination: A meta-analytic and theoretical review of quintessential self-regulatory failure. *Psychological Bulletin, 133*(1), 65–94. doi:10.1037/0033-2909.133.1.65

Tawwab, N. G. (2021). *Set boundaries, find peace: A guide to reclaiming yourself.* TarcherPerigee.

Tedeschi, R. G., & Calhoun, L. G. (2004). Posttraumatic growth: Conceptual foundations and empirical evidence. *Psychological Inquiry, 15*(1), 1–18. doi:10.1207/s15327965pli1501_01

Thoits, P. A. (2010). Stress and health: Major findings and policy implications. *Journal of Health and Social Behavior, 51*(S), S99–S112. doi:10.1177/0022146510383499

Trope, Y., & Liberman, N. (2010). Construal-level theory of psychological distance. *Psychological Review, 117*(2), 440–463. doi:10.1037/a0018963

Van der Kolk, B. A. (2014). *The body keeps the score: Brain, mind, and body in the healing of trauma.* Viking.

Walker, L. E. A. (2009). *The battered woman syndrome* (3rd ed.). Springer Publishing.

Walker, P. (2013). *Complex PTSD: From surviving to thriving.* Azure Coyote Publishing.

World Health Organization. (2019). *International statistical classification of diseases and related health problems* (11th ed.). World Health Organization.

Young, J. E., Klosko, J. S., & Weishaar, M. E. (2003). *Schema therapy: A practitioner's guide.* Guilford Press.